General American Women's Golf School
1996

The
Official Rules of
Golf

The
Official Rules of
Golf

as approved by
The United States Golf Association®
and
The Royal and Ancient Golf Club
of St. Andrews, Scotland

Effective January 1, 1996

TRIUMPH
B O O K S
CHICAGO

Typographer: Sue Knopf

For more information on the USGA®, contact:

United States Golf Association
Golf House
Far Hills, NJ 07931

The USGA On-Line
Join the USGA on the Internet at http://www.usga.org

This book is available in quantity at special discounts for your group
or organization.

For further information, contact:

Triumph Books
644 South Clark Street
Chicago, IL 60605
Tel. (312) 939-3330
Fax (312) 663-3557

PRINTED IN CANADA

User's Guide

To familiarize yourself with the Rules book, first study the Table of Contents at the front to get an idea of how the Rules are organized. Then look at the captions under each Rule to see the matters covered and the order in which they are treated. Having done this, it is hoped that most of the time you will be able to find the relevant Rule simply by reference to the Table of Contents. If not, there is an Index on pages 177–192 which should lead you to the relevant Rule.

The following suggestions are offered for learning how to apply the Rules of Golf to specific cases:

1. Identify the form of play. Match play or stroke play? The penalties differ significantly. Single, foursome or four-ball? (A foursome and a four-ball are not the same thing.) Singles match play and individual stroke play are covered in Rules 1-28. These Rules, as supplemented and modified by Rules 29-32, govern threesomes and foursomes, multi-ball match play and stroke play and bogey, par and Stableford competitions.

2. Who is involved? The player, his partner or his caddie? In match play, the player's opponent or his caddie? In stroke play, a fellow-competitor or his caddie? Or an outside agency?

3. Where did the incident occur? On the teeing ground of the hole being played? In a hazard (i.e., a bunker, a water hazard or a lateral water hazard)? On the putting green of the hole being played? Or elsewhere on the course (i.e., "through the green")? Where the incident occurs can have a significant effect on what the player may do or the relief to which he is entitled.

4. Pay attention to the Definitions set forth in full in alphabetical order at the front of the book. Definitions are repeated at the beginning of each Rule in which they are used and are likely to be important to the correct application of the Rule. Defined terms which may be significant are <u>underscored</u> the first time they appear in a Rule.

5. Carry a Rules book in your golf bag and use it whenever a question arises. Knowing the Rules may enable you not only to avoid penalties but also to save strokes.

Foreword

The United States Golf Association and the Royal and Ancient Golf Club of St. Andrews, in consultation with other golfing bodies, have carried out their customary quadrennial revision of the Rules of Golf and have agreed upon this new code to become effective January 1, 1996.

Once again no major changes have been introduced but a number of Rules have been amended in continuance of the policy of making the Rules of Golf as clear as possible. The principal changes are summarized on pages viii through xii.

The United States Golf Association and Royal and Ancient Golf Club will continue their close liaison in all matters concerning the Rules and would like to record their appreciation of the valuable assistance which they have received from other golfing bodies throughout the world.

We take this opportunity of thanking, most sincerely, our respective Committees and all those who have in many ways helped us in our endeavors.

Trey Holland
  Chairman
  Rules of Golf Committee
  United States Golf Association

John Scrivener
  Chairman
  Rules of Golf Committee
  Royal and Ancient
    Golf Club of St. Andrews

Changes Since 1995

ETIQUETTE

Pace of Play
   Restructured to highlight "pace of play" considerations.

DEFINITIONS

Ball in Play
   Amended to state that a ball in play includes a ball substituted for a ball in play whether or not such substitution is permitted. See also Rules 15-1 and 20-4.

Bunker
   Expanded to clarify that a ball is in a bunker when any part of it lies in or touches the bunker.

Casual Water
   Expanded to clarify that a ball is in casual water when it lies in or any part of it touches the casual water.

Ground Under Repair
   Expanded to clarify that stakes, when used to define ground under repair, are obstructions and that a ball is in ground under repair when any part of it lies in or touches the ground under repair.
   Additionally, Note 2 has been expanded to permit a Committee to make a Local Rule prohibiting play from an environmentally-sensitive area which has been defined as ground under repair.

Lateral Water Hazard
   Expanded to clarify that a ball is in a lateral water hazard when it lies in or any part of it touches the lateral water hazard.
   A second Note has been added permitting a Committee to make a Local Rule prohibiting play from an environmentally-sensitive area which has been defined as a lateral water hazard.

Water Hazard
   Expanded to clarify that stakes, when used to define the margins of water hazards, are obstructions and that a ball is in a water hazard when it lies in or any part of it touches the water hazard.
   A second Note has been added permitting a Committee to make a Local Rule prohibiting play from an environmentally-sensitive area which has been defined as a water hazard.

Wrong Ball
   Amended to clarify that a wrong ball is any ball other than the player's ball in play, provisional ball or second ball played under Rule 3-3 or 20-7b in stroke play. The Note has also been amended to reflect the change to the Definition of "Ball in Play."

RULES

Rule 4. Clubs; Preamble
   Amended to encourage manufacturers to submit products even if there is no reasonable basis for doubt as to its conformity with the Rules.
   A paragraph has been added providing a general statement on design and manufacturing intent, emphasizing that the intent of the design may be just as important as the finished product.

Rule 4-1. Form and Make of Clubs
Expanded to define more precisely a putter.

Rule 4-1a. General
Expanded to prohibit external attachments to a club except as otherwise permitted by the Rules.

Rule 4-1c. Grip
Amended to clarify that the grip must extend to the end of the shaft.

Rule 4-4. Maximum of Fourteen Clubs
Amended to clarify that if a player started a round with fewer than fourteen clubs he may add any number of clubs provided his total number does not exceed fourteen.

Rule 5-1. The Ball; General
A Note has been added stating that the Committee may establish a condition of a competition that the ball the player uses must be named on the current list of Conforming Golf Balls issued by the USGA.

Rule 6-7. Undue Delay; Slow Play
Expanded to address specifically "slow play."

A second Note has been added permitting a Committee to establish, in the conditions of a competition, specific pace of play guidelines and in such a condition modify the penalty for a first offense to one stroke in stroke play.

Rule 6-8. Discontinuance of Play
A Note has been added giving a Committee the authority to lay down a condition of competition requiring players to discontinue play immediately when play is suspended for a potentially dangerous situation.

Rule 7-2. Practice; During Round
Expanded to state that strokes played in continuing the play of a hole, the result of which has been decided, are not practice strokes.

Rule 8-1. Advice
Amended to clarify that the provisions of Rule 8-1 apply only during a stipulated round.

Rule 8-2a. Indicating Line of Play; Other Than on Putting Green
Expanded to state that no one may stand on an extension of the line of play beyond the hole to indicate such line while the stroke is being played.

Rule 8. Advice; Indicating Line of Play
The Note was amended to state that a team captain or coach must be identified to the Committee prior to giving advice.

Rule 13-4. Ball in Hazard
Expanded to state that the provisions of this Rule also apply when a ball which, having been lifted from a hazard, may be dropped or placed in the hazard.

Rule 14-3. Artificial Devices and Unusual Equipment; Preamble
Amended to offer manufacturers the opportunity to submit a product for a ruling without the need to believe a doubt exists as to its conformity under the Rules.

Rule 14-3. Artificial Devices and Unusual Equipment
Expanded to clarify that the use of powder or drying or moisturizing agents is permitted.

Rule 15-1. Wrong Ball; Substituted Ball; General
Amended to state that if a player substitutes a ball when not permitted, it is not a wrong ball. It becomes the ball in play under penalty of loss of hole in match play or two strokes in stroke play. See also corresponding changes to the Definition of "Ball in Play" and Rule 20-4.

Rule 19-5. Ball in Motion Deflected or Stopped; By Another Ball
Restructured into two sub-sections for clarity.

Amended to state that in clause (a.), the ball at rest (the deflecting ball) must be in play and in clause (b.) the ball in motion (the deflecting ball) must be in motion after a stroke.

Rule 20-2c(v). Dropping and Re-Dropping; When to Re-Drop
Expanded to state that if a dropped ball rolls back into the pitch-mark from which it was lifted, the ball shall be re-dropped.

Rule 20-2c(viii). Dropping and Re-Dropping; When to Re-Drop
A clause has been added to clarify that if a dropped ball comes to rest nearer the hole than where it last crossed the margin of the area or hazard under Rules 25-1(c)(i) or 25-1(c)(ii) or the margin of the water hazard or lateral water hazard under Rule 26-1 that the ball must be re-dropped.

Rule 20-3c(i). Placing and Replacing; Spot Not Determinable
Expanded to clarify that if, through the green, the spot where the ball to be placed or replaced is not determinable, the ball must be dropped through the green. See also corresponding change to Rule 25-2.

Rule 20-3d. Placing and Replacing; Ball Fails to Come to Rest on Spot
Expanded to clarify that a ball which has been placed must come to rest on that spot but does not have to remain on that spot.

Rule 20-4. When Ball Dropped or Placed Is in Play
Amended to state that a substituted ball becomes the ball in play when it has been dropped or placed. See also corresponding changes to the Definition of "Ball in Play" and Rule 15-1.

Rule 20-6. Lifting Ball Incorrectly Substituted, Dropped or Placed
Amended to allow a player who incorrectly substitutes a ball to correct the error as provided for in this Rule.

Rule 20-7. Playing from Wrong Place
Amended as a result of corresponding changes to Definition of "Ball in Play" and Rules 15-1 and 20-4.

Rule 22. Ball Interfering with or Assisting Play
The final paragraph of the Rule has been deleted referring to the accidental movement of a ball. Rule 20-1 will now apply.

Rule 23-1. Loose Impediments; Relief
Expanded to clarify that if both the ball and the loose impediment are in the same hazard, the loose impediment may not be removed.

Rule 24-1. Movable Obstructions
A Note has been added to clarify that if a player is proceeding under this Rule and the ball is not immediately recoverable, another ball may be substituted.

Rule 24-2b. Immovable Obstructions
A Note has been added to clarify that if a player is proceeding under this Rule and the ball is not immediately recoverable, another ball may be substituted.

Rule 25-1a. Casual Water, Ground Under Repair and Certain Damage to Course; Relief

A Note has been added to give a Committee the authority to make a Local Rule denying a player relief from interference with his stance from all or any of the conditions covered by this Rule.

Rule 25-1b(ii)(b). Casual Water, Ground Under Repair and Certain Damage to Course; Relief

Expanded to clarify that there is no limit to how far behind the hazard the ball may be dropped.

Rule 25-1b. Casual Water, Ground Under Repair and Certain Damage to Course

A Note has been added to clarify that if a player is proceeding under this Rule and the ball is not immediately recoverable, another ball may be substituted.

Rule 25-1c(ii)(b). Casual Water, Ground Under Repair and Certain Damage to Course

Expanded to clarify that there is no limit to how far behind the hazard the ball may be dropped.

Rule 25-2. Embedded Ball

Expanded to state that the ball when dropped must first strike a part of the course through the green. See also corresponding change to Rule 20-3c(i).

Rule 26-1c. Ball in Water Hazard

Amended to clarify that the additional options available under this clause are only available if the ball last crossed the margin of a lateral water hazard.

Restructured to reflect the addition of Rule 20-2c(viii).

Rule 26-2a. Ball Comes to Rest in the Hazard

Amended to clarify that the provisions of this Rule apply only if the ball is played from within a water hazard and comes to rest in the same hazard.

Rule 31-6. Four-Ball Stroke Play; Wrong Ball

Amended to clarify that the penalty for playing a stroke or strokes with a wrong ball is two strokes.

Rule 33-2b. The Course; New Holes

A Note has been added giving a Committee the authority to make a condition of competition that when a single round is to be played on more than one day, the holes and teeing grounds may be differently situated on each day of the competition.

Rule 34-1a. Claims and Penalties; Match Play

Expanded to state that there is no time limit on applying the penalty of disqualification if the players have agreed to waive the Rules (Rule 1-3).

Rule 34-1b. Claims and Penalties; Stroke Play

Expanded to clarify that if a competitor is advised of a breach of a Rule or a wrong handicap, between the time of returning his card and the competition closing, and the error comes to the attention of the Committee after the competition has closed, he shall be disqualified.

APPENDIX I

LOCAL RULES

Protection of Young Trees

Expanded to cover when the ball lies in a hazard. Additionally, an Exception has been added to the Local Rule prohibiting relief from a young tree if (a) it is clearly unreasonable for him to play a stroke because of interference by anything other than such tree or (b) interference by such tree would occur only through use of an unnecessarily abnormal stance, swing or direction of play.

Environmentally-Sensitive Areas

Added to provide text for a Local Rule when a Committee is required to prohibit play from environmentally-sensitive areas which are on or adjoin the course.

OPTIONAL CONDITIONS

Discontinuance of Play

Added to provide text when a Committee wishes to adopt the condition in the Note under Rule 6-8b.

Advice in Team Competitions

Amended to reflect the change to the Note under Rule 8.

APPENDIX II

Design of Clubs

Golfers interested in equipment affected by the 1988 Rules change should contact the USGA for more information.

4-1b. Alignment

A new sub-heading has been added. A new specification has also been introduced which now limits shafts from being angled forwards or backwards (along the line of play) by more than 20 degrees. Additionally, the 10 degree lie specification has been amended to apply to all clubs, not only to putters.

4-1c. Grip

Amended to indicate that a grip may have a slightly indented spiral replicating a wrapped grip. The Note has been deleted since the grace period expired January 1, 1993.

4-1d. Plain in Shape

Amended to provide clear examples of what is not considered to be plain in shape.

4-1e. Impact Area Roughness and Material

Expanded to include a new specification that requires the impact area to be of a single material, and a roughness that does not exceed decorative sandblasting or fine milling.

4-1e. Non-Metallic Club Face Markings

The specifications apply to materials that are similar in hardness to metal, e.g., ceramics.

Illustrations

Illustrations have been added or amended to depict better the meaning of the text.

APPENDIX III

The Ball; Spherical Symmetry

The actual symmetry test has been removed from the text of the Rule. That test may still be used to advise the manufacturers if the ball is not symmetrical.

Contents

Section I
Etiquette 1

Section II
Definitions 7

Section III
The Rules of Play 21

The Game

1. The Game 23
2. Match Play 24
3. Stroke Play 26

Clubs and the Ball

4. Clubs 28
5. The Ball 33

Player's Responsibilities

6. The Player 35
7. Practice 41
8. Advice; Indicating Line of Play 42
9. Information as to Strokes Taken 44

Order of Play

10. Order of Play 46

Teeing Ground

11. Teeing Ground 49

Playing the Ball

12. Searching for and Identifying Ball 51
13. Ball Played as It Lies;
    Lie, Area of Intended Swing and
    Line of Play; Stance 53
14. Striking the Ball 57
15. Wrong Ball; Substituted Ball 59

The Putting Green

16. The Putting Green 62
17. The Flagstick 65

Ball Moved, Deflected or Stopped

18. Ball at Rest Moved 67
19. Ball in Motion Deflected or Stopped 71

Relief Situations and Procedure

20. Lifting, Dropping and Placing;
    Playing from Wrong Place 75
21. Cleaning Ball 82
22. Ball Interfering with or Assisting Play 83
23. Loose Impediments 83
24. Obstructions 84
25. Abnormal Ground Conditions
    and Wrong Putting Green 88

26. Water Hazards
    (Including Lateral Water Hazards) 94
27. Ball Lost or Out of Bounds;
    Provisional Ball 98
28. Ball Unplayable 101

Other Forms of Play

29. Threesomes and Foursomes 102
30. Three-Ball, Best-Ball and
    Four-Ball Match Play 103
31. Four-Ball Stroke Play 106
32. Bogey, Par and
    Stableford Competitions 108

Administration

33. The Committee 111
34. Disputes and Decisions 115

Appendix I: Local Rules;
Conditions of the Competition 117

Local Rules

Lifting an Embedded Ball 121
Practice Between Holes 122
Marking Position of Lifted Ball 122
Prohibition Against Touching
    Line of Putt with Club 122

Protection of Young Trees 123
Environmentally-Sensitive Areas 123
Temporary Obstructions 127
"Preferred Lies" and "Winter Rules" 130

Conditions of the Competition

How to Decide Ties 133
Draw for Match Play 134
   General Numerical Draw 135
Handicap Allowances 135
Optional Conditions 136

Appendix II: Design of Clubs 141

Appendix III: The Ball 153

Appendix IV: Miscellaneous

Par Computation 159
Flagstick Dimensions 159
Protection of Persons Against Lightning 159

Rules of Amateur Status 161
   USGA Policy on Gambling 175

Index 177

SECTION I
ETIQUETTE

Courtesy on the Course

Safety

Prior to playing a stroke or making a practice swing, the player should ensure that no one is standing close by or in a position to be hit by the club, the ball or any stones, pebbles, twigs or the like which may be moved by the stroke or swing.

Consideration for Other Players

The player who has the honor should be allowed to play before his opponent or fellow-competitor tees his ball.

No one should move, talk or stand close to or directly behind the ball or the hole when a player is addressing the ball or making a stroke.

No player should play until the players in front are out of range.

Pace of Play

In the interest of all, players should play without delay.

Players searching for a ball should signal the players behind them to pass as soon as it becomes apparent that the ball will not easily be found. They should not search for five minutes before doing so. They should not continue play until the players following them have passed and are out of range.

When the play of a hole has been completed, players should immediately leave the putting green.

If a match fails to keep its place on the course and loses more than one clear hole on the players in front, it should invite the match following to pass.

Priority on the Course

In the absence of special rules, two-ball matches should have precedence over and be entitled to pass any three- or four-ball match, which should invite them through.

A single player has no standing and should give way to a match of any kind.

Any match playing a whole round is entitled to pass a match playing a shorter round.

Care of the Course

Holes in Bunkers

Before leaving a bunker, a player should carefully fill up and smooth over all holes and footprints made by him.

Replace Divots; Repair Ball-Marks and Damage by Spikes

Through the green, a player should ensure that any turf cut or displaced by him is replaced at once and pressed down and that any damage to the putting green made by a ball is carefully repaired. On completion of the hole by all players in the group, damage to the putting green caused by golf shoe spikes should be repaired.

Damage to Greens — Flagsticks, Bags, etc.

Players should ensure that, when putting down bags or the flagstick, no damage is done to the putting green and that neither they nor their caddies damage the hole by standing close to it, in handling the flagstick or in removing the ball from the hole. The flagstick should be properly replaced in the hole before the players leave the putting green. Players should not damage the putting green by leaning on their putters, particularly when removing the ball from the hole.

Golf Carts

Local notices regulating the movement of golf carts should be strictly observed.

Damage Through Practice Swings

In taking practice swings, players should avoid causing damage to the course, particularly the tees, by removing divots.

Section II
DEFINITIONS

Addressing the Ball

A player has "addressed the ball" when he has taken his <u>stance</u> and has also grounded his club, except that in a <u>hazard</u> a player has addressed the ball when he has taken his stance.

Advice

"Advice" is any counsel or suggestion which could influence a player in determining his play, the choice of a club or the method of making a <u>stroke</u>.

Information on the Rules or on matters of public information, such as the position of hazards or the flagstick on the putting green, is not advice.

Ball Deemed to Move

See "Move or Moved."

Ball Holed

See "Holed."

Ball Lost

See "Lost Ball."

Ball in Play

A ball is "in play" as soon as the player has made a <u>stroke</u> on the <u>teeing ground</u>. It remains in play until holed out, except when it is <u>lost</u>, <u>out of bounds</u> or lifted, or another ball has been substituted whether or not such substitution is permitted; a ball so substituted becomes the ball in play.

Bunker

A "bunker" is a hazard consisting of a prepared area of ground, often a hollow, from which turf or soil has been removed and replaced with sand or the like. Grass-covered ground bordering or within a bunker is not part of the bunker. The margin of a bunker extends vertically down-wards, but not upwards. A ball is in a bunker when it lies in or any part of it touches the bunker.

Caddie

A "caddie" is one who carries or handles a player's clubs during play and otherwise assists him in accordance with the Rules.

When one caddie is employed by more than one player, he is always deemed to be the caddie of the player whose ball is involved, and <u>equipment</u> carried by him is deemed to be that player's equipment, except when the caddie acts upon specific directions of another player, in which case he is considered to be that other player's caddie.

Casual Water

"Casual water" is any temporary accumulation of water on the <u>course</u> which is visible before or after the player takes his <u>stance</u> and is not in a <u>water hazard</u>. Snow and natural ice, other than frost, are either casual water or <u>loose impediments</u>, at the option of the player. Manufac-tured ice is an <u>obstruction</u>. Dew and frost are not casual water. A ball is in casual water when it lies in or any part of it touches the casual water.

Committee

Thé "Committee" is the committee in charge of the competition or, if the matter does not arise in a competi-tion, the committee in charge of the <u>course</u>.

Competitor

A "competitor" is a player in a stroke competition. A "fellow-competitor" is any person with whom the com-petitor plays. Neither is <u>partner</u> of the other.

In stroke play foursome and four-ball competitions,

where the context so admits, the word "competitor" or "fellow-competitor" includes his partner.

Course

The "course" is the whole area within which play is permitted (see Rule 33-2).

Equipment

"Equipment" is anything used, worn or carried by or for the player except any ball he has played at the hole being played and any small object, such as a coin or a tee, when used to mark the position of a ball or the extent of an area in which a ball is to be dropped. Equipment includes a golf cart, whether or not motorized. If such a cart is shared by two or more players, the cart and everything in it are deemed to be the equipment of the player whose ball is involved except that, when the cart is being moved by one of the players sharing it, the cart and everything in it are deemed to be that player's equipment.

Note: A ball played at the hole being played is equipment when it has been lifted and not put back into play.

Fellow-Competitor

See "Competitor."

Flagstick

The "flagstick" is a movable straight indicator, with or without bunting or other material attached, centered in the hole to show its position. It shall be circular in cross-section.

Forecaddie

A "forecaddie" is one who is employed by the Committee to indicate to players the position of balls during play. He is an <u>outside agency</u>.

Ground Under Repair

"Ground under repair" is any portion of the course so marked by order of the Committee or so declared by its authorized representative. It includes material piled for removal and a hole made by a greenkeeper, even if not so marked. Stakes and lines defining ground under repair are in such ground. Stakes defining ground under repair are <u>obstructions</u>. The margin of ground under repair extends vertically downwards, but not upwards. A ball is in ground under repair when it lies in or any part of it touches the ground under repair.

Note 1: Grass cuttings and other material left on the course which have been abandoned and are not intended to be removed are not ground under repair unless so marked.

Note 2: The Committee may make a Local Rule prohibiting play from ground under repair or an environmentally-sensitive area which has been defined as ground under repair.

Hazards

A "hazard" is any <u>bunker</u> or <u>water hazard</u>.

Hole

The "hole" shall be 4¼ inches (108mm) in diameter and at least 4 inches (100mm) deep. If a lining is used, it shall be sunk at least 1 inch (25mm) below the <u>putting green</u> surface unless the nature of the soil makes it impracticable to do so; its outer diameter shall not exceed 4¼ inches (108mm).

Holed

A ball is "holed" when it is at rest within the circumference of the hole and all of it is below the level of the lip of the hole.

Honor

The side entitled to play first from the <u>teeing ground</u> is said to have the "honor."

Lateral Water Hazard

A "lateral water hazard" is a <u>water hazard</u> or that part of a water hazard so situated that it is not possible or is deemed by the Committee to be impracticable to drop a ball behind the water hazard in accordance with Rule 26-1b.

That part of a water hazard to be played as a lateral water hazard should be distinctively marked. A ball is in a lateral water hazard when it lies in or any part of it touches the lateral water hazard.

Note 1: Lateral water hazards should be defined by red stakes or lines.

Note 2: The Committee may make a Local Rule prohibiting play from an environmentally-sensitive area which has been defined as a lateral water hazard.

Line of Play

The "line of play" is the direction which the player wishes his ball to take after a stroke, plus a reasonable distance on either side of the intended direction. The line of play extends vertically upwards from the ground, but does not extend beyond the hole.

Line of Putt

The "line of putt" is the line which the player wishes his ball to take after a stroke on the <u>putting green</u>. Except with respect to Rule 16-1e, the line of putt includes a reasonable distance on either side of the intended line. The line of putt does not extend beyond the hole.

Loose Impediments

"Loose impediments" are natural objects such as stones, leaves, twigs, branches and the like, dung, worms and insects and casts or heaps made by them, provided they are not fixed or growing, are not solidly embedded and do not adhere to the ball.

Sand and loose soil are loose impediments on the <u>putting green</u>, but not elsewhere.

Snow and natural ice, other than frost, are either <u>casual water</u> or loose impediments, at the option of the player. Manufactured ice is an <u>obstruction</u>.

Dew and frost are not loose impediments.

Lost Ball

A ball is "lost" if:

a. It is not found or identified as his by the player within five minutes after the player's side or his or their caddies have begun to search for it; or

b. The player has put another ball into play under the Rules, even though he may not have searched for the original ball; or

c. The player has played any stroke with a <u>provisional ball</u> from the place where the original ball is likely to be or from a point nearer the hole than that place, whereupon the provisional ball becomes the <u>ball in play</u>.

Time spent in playing a <u>wrong ball</u> is not counted in the five-minute period allowed for search.

Marker

A "marker" is one who is appointed by the Committee to record a <u>competitor's</u> score in stroke play. He may be a <u>fellow-competitor</u>. He is not a <u>referee</u>.

Matches

See "Sides and Matches."

Move or Moved

A ball is deemed to have "moved" if it leaves its position and comes to rest in any other place.

Observer

An "observer" is one who is appointed by the Committee to assist a <u>referee</u> to decide questions of fact and to report to him any breach of a Rule. An observer should not attend the flagstick, stand at or mark the position of the hole, or lift the ball or mark its position.

Obstructions

An "obstruction" is anything artificial, including the artificial surfaces and sides of roads and paths and manufactured ice, except:

a. Objects defining <u>out of bounds</u>, such as walls, fences, stakes and railings;
b. Any part of an immovable artificial object which is out of bounds; and
c. Any construction declared by the Committee to be an integral part of the course.

Out of Bounds

"Out of bounds" is ground on which play is prohibited.

When out of bounds is defined by reference to stakes or a fence or as being beyond stakes or a fence, the out of bounds line is determined by the nearest inside points of the stakes or fence posts at ground level excluding angled supports.

When out of bounds is defined by a line on the ground, the line itself is out of bounds.

The out of bounds line extends vertically upwards and downwards.

A ball is out of bounds when all of it lies out of bounds.

A player may stand out of bounds to play a ball lying within bounds.

Outside Agency

An "outside agency" is any agency not part of the match or, in stroke play, not part of the competitor's side, and includes a referee, a marker, an observer and a forecaddie. Neither wind nor water is an outside agency.

Partner

A "partner" is a player associated with another player on the same side.

In a threesome, foursome, best-ball or four-ball match, where the context so admits, the word "player" includes his partner or partners.

Penalty Stroke

A "penalty stroke" is one added to the score of a player or <u>side</u> under certain Rules. In a threesome or foursome, penalty strokes do not affect the order of play.

Provisional Ball

A "provisional ball" is a ball played under Rule 27-2 for a ball which may be <u>lost</u> outside a <u>water hazard</u> or may be <u>out of bounds</u>.

Putting Green

The "putting green" is all ground of the hole being played which is specially prepared for putting or otherwise defined as such by the Committee. A ball is on the putting green when any part of it touches the putting green.

Referee

A "referee" is one who is appointed by the Committee to accompany players to decide questions of fact and apply the Rules. He shall act on any breach of a Rule which he observes or is reported to him.

A referee should not attend the flagstick, stand at or mark the position of the hole, or lift the ball or mark its position.

Rub of the Green

A "rub of the green" occurs when a ball in motion is accidentally deflected or stopped by any <u>outside agency</u> (see Rule 19-1).

Rule

The term "Rule" includes Local Rules made by the Committee under Rule 33-8a.

Sides and Matches

Side: A player, or two or more players who are <u>partners</u>.

Single: A match in which one plays against another.

Threesome: A match in which one plays against two, and each side plays one ball.

Foursome: A match in which two play against two, and each side plays one ball.

Three-Ball: A match play competition in which three play against one another, each playing his own ball. Each player is playing two distinct matches.

Best-Ball: A match in which one plays against the better ball of two or the best ball of three players.

Four-Ball: A match in which two play their better ball against the better ball of two other players.

Stance

Taking the "stance" consists in a player placing his feet in position for and preparatory to making a <u>stroke</u>.

Stipulated Round

The "stipulated round" consists of playing the holes of the course in their correct sequence unless otherwise authorized by the Committee. The number of holes in a stipulated round is 18 unless a smaller number is authorized by the Committee. As to extension of stipulated round in match play, see Rule 2-3.

Stroke

A "stroke" is the forward movement of the club made with the intention of fairly striking at and moving the ball, but if a player checks his downswing voluntarily before the clubhead reaches the ball he is deemed not to have made a stroke.

Teeing Ground

The "teeing ground" is the starting place for the hole to be played. It is a rectangular area two club-lengths in depth, the front and the sides of which are defined by the outside limits of two tee-markers. A ball is outside the teeing ground when all of it lies outside the teeing ground.

Through the Green

"Through the green" is the whole area of the <u>course</u> except:

a. The <u>teeing ground</u> and <u>putting green</u> of the hole being played; and
b. All <u>hazards</u> on the course.

Water Hazard

A "water hazard" is any sea, lake, pond, river, ditch, surface drainage ditch or other open water course (whether or not containing water) and anything of a similar nature.

All ground or water within the margin of a water hazard is part of the water hazard. The margin of a water hazard extends vertically upwards and downwards. Stakes and lines defining the margins of water hazards are in the hazards. Such stakes are <u>obstructions</u>. A ball is in a water hazard when it lies in or any part of it touches the water hazard.

Note 1: Water hazards (other than <u>lateral water hazards</u>) should be defined by yellow stakes or lines.

Note 2: The Committee may make a Local Rule prohibiting play from an environmentally-sensitive area which has been defined as a water hazard.

Wrong Ball

A "wrong ball" is any ball other than the player's:

a. <u>Ball in play</u>,

b. <u>Provisional ball</u>, or

c. Second ball played under Rule 3-3 or Rule 20-7b in stroke play.

Note: Ball in play includes a ball substituted for the ball in play whether or not such substitution is permitted.

Section III
THE RULES OF PLAY

The Game

Rule 1 **The Game**

1-1 General

The Game of Golf consists in playing a ball from the <u>teeing ground</u> into the hole by a <u>stroke</u> or successive strokes in accordance with the Rules.

1-2 Exerting Influence on Ball

No player or caddie shall take any action to influence the position or the movement of a ball except in accordance with the Rules.

PENALTY FOR BREACH OF RULE 1-2:
Match play — Loss of hole;
Stroke play — Two strokes.

Note: In the case of a serious breach of Rule 1-2, the Committee may impose a penalty of disqualification.

1-3 Agreement to Waive Rules

Players shall not agree to exclude the operation of any Rule or to waive any penalty incurred.

PENALTY FOR BREACH OF RULE 1-3:
Match play — Disqualification of both sides;
Stroke play —Disqualification of
competitors concerned.
(Agreeing to play out of turn in stroke play — see Rule 10-2c.)

1-4 Points Not Covered by Rules

If any point in dispute is not covered by the Rules, the decision shall be made in accordance with equity.

Rule 2 | Match Play

2-1 Winner of Hole; Reckoning of Holes

In match play the game is played by holes.

Except as otherwise provided in the Rules, a hole is won by the side which holes its ball in the fewer strokes. In a handicap match the lower net score wins the hole.

The reckoning of holes is kept by the terms: so many "holes up" or "all square," and so many "to play."

A side is "dormie" when it is as many holes up as there are holes remaining to be played.

2-2 Halved Hole

A hole is halved if each side holes out in the same number of strokes.

When a player has holed out and his opponent has been left with a stroke for the half, if the player thereafter incurs a penalty, the hole is halved.

2-3 Winner of Match

A match (which consists of a <u>stipulated round</u>, unless otherwise decreed by the Committee) is won by the side which is leading by a number of holes greater than the number of holes remaining to be played.

The Committee may, for the purpose of settling a tie, extend the stipulated round to as many holes as are required for a match to be won.

2-4 Concession of Next Stroke, Hole or Match

When the opponent's ball is at rest or is deemed to be at rest under Rule 16-2, the player may concede the opponent to have holed out with his next stroke and the ball may be removed by either side with a club or otherwise.

A player may concede a hole or a match at any time prior to the conclusion of the hole or the match.

Concession of a stroke, hole or match may not be declined or withdrawn.

2-5 Claims

In match play, if a doubt or dispute arises between the players and no duly authorized representative of the Committee is available within a reasonable time, the players shall continue the match without delay. Any claim, if it is to be considered by the Committee, must be made before any player in the match plays from the next teeing ground or, in the case of the last hole of the match, before all players in the match leave the putting green.

No later claim shall be considered unless it is based on facts previously unknown to the player making the claim and the player making the claim had been given wrong information (Rules 6-2a and 9) by an opponent. In any case, no later claim shall be considered after the result of the match has been officially announced, unless the Committee is satisfied that the opponent knew he was giving wrong information.

2-6 General Penalty

The penalty for a breach of a Rule in match play is loss of hole except when otherwise provided.

Rule 3   **Stroke Play**

3-1   **Winner**

The competitor who plays the <u>stipulated round</u> or rounds in the fewest strokes is the winner.

3-2   **Failure to Hole Out**

If a competitor fails to hole out at any hole and does not correct his mistake before he plays a <u>stroke</u> from the next <u>teeing ground</u> or, in the case of the last hole of the round, before he leaves the <u>putting green</u>, *he shall be disqualified.*

3-3   **Doubt as to Procedure**

a. PROCEDURE

In stroke play only, when during play of a hole a competitor is doubtful of his rights or procedure, he may, without penalty, play a second ball. After the situation which caused the doubt has arisen, the competitor should, before taking further action, announce to his marker or a fellow-competitor his decision to invoke this Rule and the ball with which he will score if the Rules permit.

The competitor shall report the facts to the <u>Committee</u> before returning his score card unless he scores the same with both balls; if he fails to do so, he shall be disqualified.

b. DETERMINATION OF SCORE FOR HOLE

If the Rules allow the procedure selected in advance by the competitor, the score with the ball selected shall be his score for the hole.

If the competitor fails to announce in advance

his decision to invoke this Rule or his selection, the score with the original ball or, if the original ball is not one of the balls being played, the first ball put into play shall count if the Rules allow the procedure adopted for such ball.

Note: A second ball played under Rule 3-3 is not a provisional ball under Rule 27-2.

3-4 **Refusal to Comply with a Rule**

If a competitor refuses to comply with a Rule affecting the rights of another competitor, *he shall be disqualified.*

3-5 **General Penalty**

The penalty for a breach of a Rule in stroke play is two strokes except when otherwise provided.

Clubs and the Ball

The United States Golf Association and the Royal and Ancient Golf Club of St. Andrews reserve the right to change the Rules and make and change the interpretations relating to clubs, balls and other implements at any time.

Rule 4 Clubs

A player in doubt as to the conformity of a club should consult the United States Golf Association.

A manufacturer may submit to the United States Golf Association a sample of a club which is to be manufactured for a ruling as to whether the club conforms with Rule 4 and Appendix II. Such sample will become the property of the United States Golf Association for reference purposes. If a manufacturer fails to submit a sample before manufacturing and/or marketing the club, he assumes the risk of a ruling that the club does not conform with the Rules of Golf.

Where a club, or part of a club, is required to have some specific property, this means that it must be designed and manufactured with the intention of having that property. The finished club or part must have that property within manufacturing tolerances appropriate to the material used.

4-1 Form and Make of Clubs

A club is an implement designed to be used for striking the ball.

A putter is a club with a loft not exceeding ten degrees designed primarily for use on the putting green.

The player's clubs shall conform with the provisions of this Rule and with the specifications and interpretations set forth in Appendix II.

a. GENERAL

The club shall be composed of a shaft and a head. All parts of the club shall be fixed so that the club is one unit. The club shall not be designed to be adjustable except for weight (see also Appendix II). The club shall not be substantially different from the traditional and customary form and make, and shall have no external attachments except as otherwise permitted by the Rules.

b. SHAFT

The shaft shall be straight, with the same bending and twisting properties in any direction, and shall be attached to the clubhead at the heel either directly or through a single plain neck and/or socket. A putter shaft may be attached to any point in the head.

c. GRIP

The grip consists of that part of the shaft designed to be held by the player and any material added to it for the purpose of obtaining a firm hold. The grip shall be straight and plain in form, shall extend to the end of the shaft and shall not be molded for any part of the hands.

d. CLUBHEAD

The distance from the heel to the toe of the clubhead shall be greater than the distance from the face to the back. The clubhead shall be generally plain in shape.

The clubhead shall have only one striking face, except that a putter may have two such faces if their characteristics are the same, and they are opposite each other.

e. CLUB FACE

The face of the club shall be hard and rigid (some exceptions may be made for putters) and, except for such markings as are permitted by Appendix II, shall be smooth and shall not have any degree of concavity.

f. WEAR AND ALTERATION

A club which conforms with Rule 4-1 when new is deemed to conform after wear through normal use. Any part of a club which has been purposely altered is regarded as new and must conform, in the altered state, with the Rules.

g. DAMAGE

If a player's club ceases to conform with Rule 4-1 because of damage sustained in the normal course of play, the player may:

(i)   use the club in its damaged state, but only for the remainder of the <u>stipulated round</u> during which such damage was sustained; or

(ii) without unduly delaying play, repair it.

A club which ceases to conform because of damage sustained other than in the normal course of play shall not subsequently be used during the round.

(Damage changing playing characteristics of club — see Rule 4-2.)

(Damage rendering club unfit for play — see
Rule 4-4a.)

4-2 Playing Characteristics Changed

During a <u>stipulated round</u>, the playing characteristics of a club shall not be purposely changed
by adjustment or by any other means.

If the playing characteristics of a player's club are
changed during a round because of damage sustained in the normal course of play, the player may:

    (i) use the club in its altered state; or

    (ii) without unduly delaying play, repair it.

If the playing characteristics of a player's club are
changed because of damage sustained other than in
the normal course of play, the club shall not subsequently be used during the round.

Damage to a club which occurred prior to a
round may be repaired during the round, provided
the playing characteristics are not changed and
play is not unduly delayed.

4-3 Foreign Material

Foreign material must not be applied to the club
face for the purpose of influencing the movement
of the ball.

PENALTY FOR BREACH OF RULE 4-1, -2 OR -3:
Disqualification.

4-4 Maximum of Fourteen Clubs

a. SELECTION AND REPLACEMENT OF CLUBS

The player shall start a <u>stipulated round</u> with
not more than fourteen clubs. He is limited to
the clubs thus selected for that round except

that, without unduly delaying play, he may:

    (i) if he started with fewer than fourteen clubs, add any number provided his total number does not exceed fourteen; and

    (ii) replace, with any club, a club which becomes unfit for play in the normal course of play.

The addition or replacement of a club or clubs may not be made by borrowing any club selected for play by any other person playing on the course.

b. PARTNERS MAY SHARE CLUBS

Partners may share clubs, provided that the total number of clubs carried by the partners so sharing does not exceed fourteen.

PENALTY FOR BREACH OF RULE 4-4a OR b, REGARDLESS OF NUMBER OF EXCESS CLUBS CARRIED:

Match play — At the conclusion of the hole at which the breach is discovered, the state of the match shall be adjusted by deducting one hole for each hole at which a breach occurred. Maximum deduction per round: two holes.

Stroke play — Two strokes for each hole at which any breach occurred; maximum penalty per round: four strokes.

Bogey and par competitions — Penalties as in match play.

Stableford competitions — see Note to Rule 32-1b.

c. EXCESS CLUB DECLARED OUT OF PLAY

Any club carried or used in breach of this Rule shall be declared out of play by the player immedi-

ately upon discovery that a breach has occurred
and thereafter shall not be used by the player during the round.

PENALTY FOR BREACH OF RULE 4-4c:
Disqualification.

Rule 5   **The Ball**

5-1   **General**

The ball the player uses shall conform to
requirements specified in Appendix III on maximum weight, minimum size, spherical symmetry,
initial velocity and overall distance.

Note: The Committee may require, in the conditions of a competition (Rule 33-1), that the ball
the player uses must be named on the current List
of Conforming Golf Balls issued by the United
States Golf Association.

5-2   **Foreign Material**

Foreign material must not be applied to a ball for
the purpose of changing its playing characteristics.

PENALTY FOR BREACH OF RULE 5-1 OR 5-2:
Disqualification.

5-3   **Ball Unfit for Play**

A ball is unfit for play if it is visibly cut, cracked
or out of shape. A ball is not unfit for play solely
because mud or other materials adhere to it, its
surface is scratched or scraped or its paint is damaged or discolored.

If a player has reason to believe his ball has become
unfit for play during the play of the hole being
played, he may during the play of such hole lift his

ball without penalty to determine whether it is unfit.

Before lifting the ball, the player must announce his intention to his opponent in match play or his marker or a fellow-competitor in stroke play and mark the position of the ball. He may then lift and examine the ball without cleaning it and must give his opponent, marker or fellow-competitor an opportunity to examine the ball.

If he fails to comply with this procedure, *he shall incur a penalty of one stroke.*

If it is determined that the ball has become unfit for play during play of the hole being played, the player may substitute another ball, placing it on the spot where the original ball lay. Otherwise, the original ball shall be replaced.

If a ball breaks into pieces as a result of a stroke, the stroke shall be cancelled and the player shall play a ball without penalty as nearly as possible at the spot from which the original ball was played (see Rule 20-5).

*PENALTY FOR BREACH OF RULE 5-3:
Match play — Loss of hole;
Stroke play — Two strokes.
*If a player incurs the general penalty
for breach of Rule 5-3, no additional penalty
under the Rule shall be applied.

Note: If the opponent, marker or fellow-competitor wishes to dispute a claim of unfitness, he must do so before the player plays another ball.

(Cleaning ball lifted from putting green or under any other Rule — see Rule 21.)

Player's Responsibilities

Rule 6   **The Player**

Definition

A "marker" is one who is appointed by the Committee to record a <u>competitor's</u> score in stroke play. He may be a <u>fellow-competitor</u>. He is not a <u>referee</u>.

6-1   **Conditions of Competition**

The player is responsible for knowing the conditions under which the competition is to be played (Rule 33-1).

6-2   **Handicap**

a. MATCH PLAY

Before starting a match in a handicap competition, the players should determine from one another their respective handicaps. If a player begins the match having declared a higher handicap which would affect the number of strokes given or received, *he shall be disqualified*; otherwise, the player shall play off the declared handicap.

b. STROKE PLAY

In any round of a handicap competition, the competitor shall ensure that his handicap is recorded on his score card before it is returned to the Committee. If no handicap is recorded on his score card before it is returned, or if the recorded handicap is higher than that to which he is entitled and this affects the number of strokes received, *he shall be disqualified* from that round of the handicap competition; otherwise, the score shall stand.

Note: It is the player's responsibility to know the holes at which handicap strokes are to be given or received.

6-3 Time of Starting and Groups

a. TIME OF STARTING

The player shall start at the time laid down by the Committee.

b. GROUPS

In stroke play, the competitor shall remain throughout the round in the group arranged by the Committee unless the Committee authorizes or ratifies a change.

PENALTY FOR BREACH OF RULE 6-3:
Disqualification.

(Best-ball and four-ball play — see Rules 30-3a and 31-2.)

Note: The Committee may provide in the conditions of a competition (Rule 33-1) that, if the player arrives at his starting point, ready to play, within five minutes after his starting time, in the absence of circumstances which warrant waiving the penalty of disqualification as provided in Rule 33-7, the penalty for failure to start on time is *loss of the first hole in match play or two strokes at the first hole in stroke play* instead of disqualification.

6-4 Caddie

The player may have only one <u>caddie</u> at any one time, *under penalty of disqualification.*

For any breach of a Rule by his caddie, the player incurs the applicable penalty.

6-5 **Ball**

The responsibility for playing the proper ball rests with the player. Each player should put an identification mark on his ball.

6-6 **Scoring in Stroke Play**

a. RECORDING SCORES

After each hole the <u>marker</u> should check the score with the competitor and record it. On completion of the round the marker shall sign the card and hand it to the competitor. If more than one marker records the scores, each shall sign for the part for which he is responsible.

b. SIGNING AND RETURNING CARD

After completion of the round, the competitor should check his score for each hole and settle any doubtful points with the Committee. He shall ensure that the marker has signed the card, countersign the card himself and return it to the Committee as soon as possible.

PENALTY FOR BREACH OF RULE 6-6b:
Disqualification.

c. ALTERATION OF CARD

No alteration may be made on a card after the competitor has returned it to the Committee.

d. WRONG SCORE FOR HOLE

The competitor is responsible for the correctness of the score recorded for each hole on his card. If he returns a score for any hole lower than actually taken, *he shall be disqualified.* If he returns a score for any hole higher than actually taken, the score as returned shall stand.

Note 1: The Committee is responsible for the addition of scores and application of the handicap recorded on the card — see Rule 33-5.

Note 2: In four-ball stroke play, see also Rule 31-4 and -7a.

6-7 **Undue Delay; Slow Play**

The player shall play without undue delay and in accordance with any pace of play guidelines which may be laid down by the Committee. Between completion of a hole and playing from the next teeing ground, the player shall not unduly delay play.

PENALTY FOR BREACH OF RULE 6-7:
Match play — Loss of hole;
Stroke play — Two strokes.
For subsequent offense — Disqualification.

Note 1: If the player unduly delays play between holes, he is delaying the play of the next hole and the penalty applies to that hole.

Note 2: For the purpose of preventing slow play, the Committee may, in the conditions of a competition (Rule 33-1), lay down pace of play guidelines including maximum periods of time allowed to complete a stipulated round, a hole or a stroke.

In stroke play only, the Committee may, in such a condition, modify the penalty for a breach of this Rule as follows:
First offense — One stroke;
Second offense — Two strokes.
For subsequent offense — Disqualification.

6-8 **Discontinuance of Play**

a. WHEN PERMITTED

The player shall not discontinue play unless:

(i) the Committee has suspended play;

(ii) he believes there is danger from lightning;

(iii) he is seeking a decision from the Committee on a doubtful or disputed point (see Rules 2-5 and 34-3); or

(iv) there is some other good reason such as sudden illness.

Bad weather is not of itself a good reason for discontinuing play.

If the player discontinues play without specific permission from the Committee, he shall report to the Committee as soon as practicable. If he does so and the Committee considers his reason satisfactory, the player incurs no penalty. Otherwise, *the player shall be disqualified.*

Exception in match play: Players discontinuing match play by agreement are not subject to disqualification unless by so doing the competition is delayed.

Note: Leaving the course does not of itself constitute discontinuance of play.

b. PROCEDURE WHEN PLAY SUSPENDED
BY COMMITTEE

When play is suspended by the Committee, if the players in a match or group are between the play of two holes, they shall not resume play until the Committee has ordered a resumption of play. If they are in the process of playing a hole, they may continue provided they do so without delay. If they choose to continue, they shall discontinue either before or immediately after completing the hole, and shall not thereafter resume play until the Committee has ordered a resumption of play.

When play has been suspended by the Committee, the player shall resume play when the Committee has ordered a resumption of play.

PENALTY FOR BREACH OF RULE 6-8b:
Disqualification.

Note: The Committee may provide in the conditions of a competition (Rule 33-1) that, in potentially dangerous situations, play shall be discontinued immediately following a suspension of play by the Committee. If a player fails to discontinue play immediately, he shall be disqualified unless circumstances warrant waiving such penalty as provided in Rule 33-7.

(Resumption of play — see Rule 33-2d.)

c. LIFTING BALL WHEN PLAY DISCONTINUED

When during the play of a hole a player discontinues play under Rule 6-8a, he may lift his ball. A ball may be cleaned when so lifted. If a ball has been so lifted, the player shall, when play is resumed, place a ball on the spot from which the original ball was lifted.

PENALTY FOR BREACH OF RULE 6-8c:
Match play — Loss of hole;
Stroke play — Two strokes.

Rule 7   Practice

7-1   Before or Between Rounds

a. MATCH PLAY

On any day of a match play competition, a player may practice on the competition <u>course</u> before a round.

b. STROKE PLAY

On any day of a stroke competition or play-off, a competitor shall not practice on the competition <u>course</u> or test the surface of any putting green on the course before a round or play-off. When two or more rounds of a stroke competition are to be played over consecutive days, practice between those rounds on any competition course remaining to be played is prohibited.

Exception: Practice putting or chipping on or near the first <u>teeing ground</u> before starting a round or play-off is permitted.

PENALTY FOR BREACH OF RULE 7-1b:
Disqualification.

Note: The Committee may in the conditions of a competition (Rule 33-1) prohibit practice on the competition course on any day of a match play competition or permit practice on the competition course or part of the course (Rule 33-2c) on any day of or between rounds of a stroke competition.

7-2   During Round

A player shall not play a practice <u>stroke</u> either during the play of a hole or between the play of

---

two holes except that, between the play of two holes, the player may practice putting or chipping on or near the <u>putting green</u> of the hole last played, any practice putting green or the <u>teeing ground</u> of the next hole to be played in the round, provided such practice stroke is not played from a hazard and does not unduly delay play (Rule 6-7).

Strokes played in continuing the play of a hole, the result of which has been decided, are not practice strokes.

Exception: When play has been suspended by the Committee, a player may, prior to resumption of play, practice (a) as provided in this Rule, (b) anywhere other than on the competition course and (c) as otherwise permitted by the Committee.

PENALTY FOR BREACH OF RULE 7-2:
Match play — Loss of hole;
Stroke play — Two strokes.
In the event of a breach between the play of two holes,
the penalty applies to the next hole.

Note 1: A practice swing is not a practice stroke and may be taken at any place, provided the player does not breach the Rules.

Note 2: The Committee may prohibit practice on or near the <u>putting green</u> of the hole last played.

Rule 8	**Advice; Indicating Line of Play**

Definitions

"Advice" is any counsel or suggestion which could influence a player in determining his play, the

---

choice of a club or the method of making a <u>stroke</u>.

Information on the Rules or on matters of public information, such as the position of hazards or the flagstick on the putting green, is not advice.

The "line of play" is the direction which the player wishes his ball to take after a stroke, plus a reasonable distance on either side of the intended direction. The line of play extends vertically upwards from the ground, but does not extend beyond the hole.

8-1 **Advice**

During a <u>stipulated round</u>, a player shall not give <u>advice</u> to anyone in the competition except his partner. A player may ask for advice during a stipulated round from only his partner or either of their caddies.

8-2 **Indicating Line of Play**

a. OTHER THAN ON PUTTING GREEN

Except on the <u>putting green</u>, a player may have the <u>line of play</u> indicated to him by anyone, but no one shall be positioned by the player on or close to the line or an extension of the line beyond the hole while the <u>stroke</u> is being played. Any mark placed during the play of a hole by the player or with his knowledge to indicate the line shall be removed before the stroke is played.

Exception: Flagstick attended or held up — see Rule 17-1.

b. ON THE PUTTING GREEN

When the player's ball is on the <u>putting green</u>, the player, his partner or either of their caddies may, before but not during the <u>stroke</u>, point out a line for putting, but in so doing the putting green shall not be touched. No mark shall be placed anywhere to indicate a line for putting.

PENALTY FOR BREACH OF RULE:
Match play — Loss of hole;
Stroke play — Two strokes.

Note: The Committee may, in the conditions of a team competition (Rule 33-1), permit each team to appoint one person who may give <u>advice</u> (including pointing out a line for putting) to members of that team. The Committee may lay down conditions relating to the appointment and permitted conduct of such person, who must be identified to the Committee before giving advice.

Rule 9 Information as to Strokes Taken

9-1 General

The number of strokes a player has taken shall include any penalty strokes incurred.

9-2 Match Play

A player who has incurred a penalty shall inform his opponent as soon as practicable, unless he is obviously proceeding under a Rule involving a penalty and this has been observed by his opponent. If he fails so to inform his opponent, he shall be deemed to have given wrong information, even if he was not aware that he had incurred a penalty.

An opponent is entitled to ascertain from the player, during the play of a hole, the number of strokes he has taken and, after play of a hole, the number of strokes taken on the hole just completed.

If during the play of a hole the player gives or is deemed to give wrong information as to the number of strokes taken, he shall incur no penalty if he corrects the mistake before his opponent has played his next stroke. If the player fails so to correct the wrong information, *he shall lose the hole*.

If after play of a hole the player gives or is deemed to give wrong information as to the number of strokes taken on the hole just completed and this affects the opponent's understanding of the result of the hole, he shall incur no penalty if he corrects his mistake before any player plays from the next <u>teeing ground</u> or, in the case of the last hole of the match, before all players leave the <u>putting green</u>. If the player fails so to correct the wrong information, *he shall lose the hole*.

9-3 **Stroke Play**

A competitor who has incurred a penalty should inform his marker as soon as practicable.

Order of Play

Rule 10   **Order of Play**

10-1   **Match Play**

a. Teeing Ground

The side entitled to play first from the <u>teeing ground</u> is said to have the "honor."

The side which shall have the honor at the first teeing ground shall be determined by the order of the draw. In the absence of a draw, the honor should be decided by lot.

The side which wins a hole shall take the honor at the next teeing ground. If a hole has been halved, the side which had the honor at the previous teeing ground shall retain it.

b. Other Than on Teeing Ground

When the balls are in play, the ball farther from the hole shall be played first. If the balls are equidistant from the hole, the ball to be played first should be decided by lot.

Exception: Rule 30-3c (best-ball and four-ball match play).

c. Playing Out of Turn

If a player plays when his opponent should have played, the opponent may immediately require the player to cancel the stroke so played and, in correct order, play a ball without penalty as nearly as possible at the spot from which the original ball was last played (see Rule 20-5).

10-2 Stroke Play

a. Teeing Ground

The competitor entitled to play first from the <u>teeing ground</u> is said to have the "honor."

The competitor who shall have the honor at the first teeing ground shall be determined by the order of the draw. In the absence of a draw, the honor should be decided by lot.

The competitor with the lowest score at a hole shall take the honor at the next teeing ground. The competitor with the second lowest score shall play next and so on. If two or more competitors have the same score at a hole, they shall play from the next teeing ground in the same order as at the previous teeing ground.

b. Other Than on Teeing Ground

When the balls are in play, the ball farthest from the hole shall be played first. If two or more balls are equidistant from the hole, the ball to be played first should be decided by lot.

Exceptions: Rules 22 (ball interfering with or assisting play) and 31-5 (four-ball stroke play).

c. Playing Out of Turn

If a competitor plays out of turn, no penalty is incurred and the ball shall be played as it lies. If, however, the Committee determines that competitors have agreed to play in an order other than that set forth in Clauses 2a and 2b of this Rule to give one of them an advantage, *they shall be disqualified.*

(Incorrect order of play in threesomes and foursomes stroke play — see Rule 29-3.)

10-3 Provisional Ball or Second Ball from Teeing Ground

If a player plays a <u>provisional ball</u> or a second ball from a <u>teeing ground</u>, he should do so after his opponent or fellow-competitor has played his first <u>stroke</u>. If a player plays a provisional ball or a second ball out of turn, Clauses 1c and 2c of this Rule shall apply.

10-4 Ball Moved in Measuring

If a ball is moved in measuring to determine which ball is farther from the hole, no penalty is incurred and the ball shall be replaced.

Teeing Ground

Rule 11   **Teeing Ground**

Definition

The "teeing ground" is the starting place for the hole to be played. It is a rectangular area two club-lengths in depth, the front and the sides of which are defined by the outside limits of two tee-markers. A ball is outside the teeing ground when all of it lies outside the teeing ground.

11-1   **Teeing**

In teeing, the ball may be placed on the ground, on an irregularity of surface created by the player on the ground or on a tee, sand or other substance in order to raise it off the ground.

A player may stand outside the <u>teeing ground</u> to play a ball within it.

11-2   **Tee-Markers**

Before a player plays his first stroke with any ball from the teeing ground of the hole being played, the tee-markers are deemed to be fixed. In such circumstances, if the player moves or allows to be moved a tee-marker for the purpose of avoiding interference with his stance, the area of his intended swing or his line of play, *he shall incur the penalty for a breach of Rule 13-2.*

11-3   **Ball Falling Off Tee**

If a ball, when not <u>in play</u>, falls off a tee or is knocked off a tee by the player in addressing it, it may be re-teed without penalty, but if a <u>stroke</u> is made at the ball in these circumstances, whether the ball is moving or not, the stroke counts but no penalty is incurred.

11-4 Playing from Outside Teeing Ground

a. MATCH PLAY

If a player, when starting a hole, plays a ball from outside the <u>teeing ground</u>, the opponent may immediately require the player to cancel the stroke so played and play a ball from within the teeing ground, without penalty.

b. STROKE PLAY

If a competitor, when starting a hole, plays a ball from outside the <u>teeing ground</u>, *he shall incur a penalty of two strokes* and shall then play a ball from within the teeing ground.

If the competitor plays a stroke from the next teeing ground without first correcting his mistake or, in the case of the last hole of the round, leaves the <u>putting green</u> without first declaring his intention to correct his mistake, *he shall be disqualified.*

Strokes played by a competitor from outside the teeing ground do not count in his score.

11-5 Playing from Wrong Teeing Ground
The provisions of Rule 11-4 apply.

Playing the Ball

Rule 12 **Searching for and Identifying Ball**

Definitions

A "hazard" is any <u>bunker</u> or <u>water hazard</u>.

A "bunker" is a <u>hazard</u> consisting of a prepared area of ground, often a hollow, from which turf or soil has been removed and replaced with sand or the like. Grass-covered ground bordering or within a bunker is not part of the bunker. The margin of a bunker extends vertically downwards, but not upwards. A ball is in a bunker when it lies in or any part of it touches the bunker.

A "water hazard" is any sea, lake, pond, river, ditch, surface drainage ditch or other open water course (whether or not containing water) and anything of a similar nature.

All ground or water within the margin of a water hazard is part of the water hazard. The margin of a water hazard extends vertically upwards and downwards. Stakes and lines defining the margins of water hazards are in the hazards. Such stakes are <u>obstructions</u>. A ball is in a water hazard when it lies in or any part of it touches the water hazard.

12-1 **Searching for Ball; Seeing Ball**

In searching for his ball anywhere on the course, the player may touch or bend long grass, rushes, bushes, whins, heather or the like, but only to the extent necessary to find and identify it, provided that this does not improve the lie of the ball, the area of his intended swing or his line of play.

A player is not necessarily entitled to see his ball

when playing a stroke.

In a <u>hazard,</u> if a ball is covered by <u>loose impediments</u> or sand, the player may remove by probing, raking or other means as much thereof as will enable him to see a part of the ball. If an excess is removed, no penalty is incurred and the ball shall be re-covered so that only a part of the ball is visible. If the ball is moved in such removal, no penalty is incurred; the ball shall be replaced and, if necessary, re-covered. As to removal of loose impediments outside a hazard, see Rule 23.

If a ball lying in <u>casual water</u>, <u>ground under repair</u> or a hole, cast or runway made by a burrowing animal, a reptile or a bird is accidentally moved during search, no penalty is incurred; the ball shall be replaced, unless the player elects to proceed under Rule 25-1b.

If a ball is believed to be lying in water in a <u>water hazard</u>, the player may probe for it with a club or otherwise. If the ball is moved in so doing, no penalty is incurred; the ball shall be replaced, unless the player elects to proceed under Rule 26-1.

PENALTY FOR BREACH OF RULE 12-1:
Match play — Loss of hole;
Stroke play — Two strokes.

12-2 **Identifying Ball**

The responsibility for playing the proper ball rests with the player. Each player should put an identification mark on his ball.

Except in a <u>hazard</u>, the player may, without penalty, lift a ball he believes to be his own for the purpose of identification and clean it to the extent necessary for identification. If the ball is the player's ball, he shall replace it. Before lifting the ball, the player must announce his intention to his opponent in match play or his marker or a fellow-competitor in stroke play and mark the position of the ball. He must then give his opponent, marker or fellow-competitor an opportunity to observe the lifting and replacement. If he lifts his ball without announcing his intention in advance, marking the position of the ball or giving his opponent, marker or fellow-competitor an opportunity to observe, or if he lifts his ball for identification in a hazard, or cleans it more than necessary for identification, *he shall incur a penalty of one stroke* and the ball shall be replaced.

If a player who is required to replace a ball fails to do so, *he shall incur the penalty* for a breach of Rule 20-3a, but no additional penalty under Rule 12-2 shall be applied.

Rule 13 Ball Played as It Lies; Lie, Area of Intended Swing and Line of Play; Stance

Definitions

A "hazard" is any <u>bunker</u> or <u>water hazard.</u>

A "bunker" is a <u>hazard</u> consisting of a prepared area of ground, often a hollow, from which turf or soil has been removed and replaced with sand or the like. Grass-covered ground bordering or within a bunker is not part of the bunker. The margin of a bunker extends vertically downwards, but not upwards. A ball is in a bunker when it lies in or any part of it touches the bunker.

A "water hazard" is any sea, lake, pond, river,

ditch, surface drainage ditch or other open water course (whether or not containing water) and anything of a similar nature.

All ground or water within the margin of a water hazard is part of the water hazard. The margin of a water hazard extends vertically upwards and downwards. Stakes and lines defining the margins of water hazards are in the hazards. Such stakes are <u>obstructions</u>. A ball is in a water hazard when it lies in or any part of it touches the water hazard.

The "line of play" is the direction which the player wishes his ball to take after a stroke, plus a reasonable distance on either side of the intended direction. The line of play extends vertically upwards from the ground, but does not extend beyond the hole.

13-1 **Ball Played as It Lies**

The ball shall be played as it lies, except as otherwise provided in the Rules.

(Ball at rest moved — see Rule 18.)

13-2 **Improving Lie, Area of Intended Swing or Line of Play**

Except as provided in the Rules, a player shall not improve or allow to be improved:

the position or lie of his ball,

the area of his intended swing,

his <u>line of play</u> or a reasonable extension of that line beyond the hole or

the area in which he is to drop or place a ball

by any of the following actions:

moving, bending or breaking anything growing or fixed (including immovable
<u>obstructions</u> and objects defining <u>out of</u>
<u>bounds</u>) or

removing or pressing down sand, loose soil,
replaced divots, other cut turf placed in
position or other irregularities of surface
except as follows:

as may occur in fairly taking his <u>stance</u>,
in making a <u>stroke</u> or the backward movement of his club for a stroke,
on the <u>teeing ground</u> in creating or eliminat-
ing irregularities of surface, or
on the <u>putting green</u> in removing sand and
loose soil as provided in Rule 16-1a or in
repairing damage as provided in Rule 16-1c.
The club may be grounded only lightly and
shall not be pressed on the ground.

Exception: Ball in hazard — see Rule 13-4.

13-3 **Building Stance**
A player is entitled to place his feet firmly in taking his stance, but he shall not build a stance.

13-4 **Ball Lying in or Touching Hazard**
Except as provided in the Rules, before making a
<u>stroke</u> at a ball which is in a <u>hazard</u> (whether a
<u>bunker</u> or a <u>water hazard</u>) or which, having been
lifted from a hazard, may be dropped or placed in
the hazard, the player shall not:

a. Test the condition of the hazard or any similar
hazard,

b. Touch the ground in the hazard or water in the water hazard with a club or otherwise, or

c. Touch or move a <u>loose impediment</u> lying in or touching the hazard.

Exceptions:

1. Provided nothing is done which constitutes testing the condition of the hazard or improves the lie of the ball, there is no penalty if the player (a) touches the ground in any hazard or water in a water hazard as a result of or to prevent falling, in removing an <u>obstruction</u>, in measuring or in retrieving or lifting a ball under any Rule or (b) places his clubs in a hazard.

2. The player after playing the stroke, or his <u>caddie</u> at any time without the authority of the player, may smooth sand or soil in the hazard, provided that, if the ball is still in the hazard, nothing is done which improves the lie of the ball or assists the player in his subsequent play of the hole.

Note: At any time, including at address or in the backward movement for the stroke, the player may touch with a club or otherwise any obstruction, any construction declared by the Committee to be an integral part of the course or any grass, bush, tree or other growing thing.

PENALTY FOR BREACH OF RULE:
Match play — Loss of hole;
Stroke play — Two strokes.

(Searching for ball — see Rule 12-1.)

Rule 14   **Striking the Ball**

Definition

A "stroke" is the forward movement of the club made with the intention of fairly striking at and moving the ball, but if a player checks his down-swing voluntarily before the clubhead reaches the ball he is deemed not to have made a stroke.

14-1   **Ball to Be Fairly Struck At**

The ball shall be fairly struck at with the head of the club and must not be pushed, scraped or spooned.

14-2   **Assistance**

In making a <u>stroke</u>, a player shall not accept physical assistance or protection from the elements.

PENALTY FOR BREACH OF RULE 14-1 OR -2:
Match play — Loss of hole;
Stroke play — Two strokes.

14-3   **Artificial Devices and Unusual Equipment**

A player in doubt as to whether use of an item would constitute a breach of Rule 14-3 should consult the United States Golf Association.

A manufacturer may submit to the United States Golf Association a sample of an item which is to be manufactured for a ruling as to whether its use during a stipulated round would cause a player to be in breach of Rule 14-3. Such sample will become the property of the United States Golf Association for reference purposes. If a manufacturer fails to submit a sample before manufacturing and/or marketing the item, he assumes the risk of a ruling that use of the item would be contrary to the Rules of Golf.

Except as provided in the Rules, during a stipulated round the player shall not use any artificial device or unusual equipment:

a. Which might assist him in making a stroke or in his play; or

b. For the purpose of gauging or measuring distance or conditions which might affect his play; or

c. Which might assist him in gripping the club, except that:
   (i) plain gloves may be worn:
   (ii) resin, powder and drying or moisturizing agents may be used;
   (iii) tape or gauze may be applied to the grip (provided such application does not render the grip non-conforming under Rule 4-1c); and
   (iv) a towel or handkerchief may be wrapped around the grip.

PENALTY FOR BREACH OF RULE 14-3:
Disqualification.

14-4 **Striking the Ball More than Once**

If a player's club strikes the ball more than once in the course of a <u>stroke</u>, the player shall count the stroke and *add a penalty stroke*, making two strokes in all.

14-5 **Playing Moving Ball**

A player shall not play while his ball is moving.

Exceptions:

Ball falling off tee — Rule 11-3.

Striking the ball more than once — Rule 14-4.

Ball moving in water — Rule 14-6.

When the ball begins to move only after the player has begun the <u>stroke</u> or the backward movement of his club for the stroke, he shall incur no penalty under this Rule for playing a moving ball, but he is not exempt from any penalty incurred under the following Rules:

Ball at rest moved by player — Rule 18-2a.

Ball at rest moving after address — Rule 18-2b.

Ball at rest moving after loose impediment touched — Rule 18-2c.

(Ball purposely deflected or stopped by player, partner or caddie — see Rule 1-2.)

14-6 **Ball Moving in Water**

When a ball is moving in water in a <u>water hazard</u>, the player may, without penalty, make a <u>stroke</u>, but he must not delay making his stroke in order to allow the wind or current to improve the position of the ball. A ball moving in water in a water hazard may be lifted if the player elects to invoke Rule 26.

> **PENALTY FOR BREACH OF RULE 14-5 OR -6:**
> *Match play — Loss of hole;*
> *Stroke play — Two strokes.*

Rule 15 **Wrong Ball; Substituted Ball**

Definition

A "wrong ball" is any ball other than the player's:

a. <u>Ball in play,</u>

b. <u>Provisional ball</u> or

c. Second ball played under Rule 3-3 or Rule 20-7b in stroke play.

Note: Ball in play includes a ball substituted for the ball in play, whether or not such substitution is permitted.

15-1 **General**

A player must hole out with the ball played from the <u>teeing ground</u> unless a Rule permits him to substitute another ball. If a player substitutes another ball when not so permitted, that ball is not a <u>wrong ball</u>; it becomes the <u>ball in play</u> and, if the error is not corrected as provided in Rule 20-6, *the player shall incur a penalty of loss of hole in match play or two strokes in stroke play.*

(Playing from wrong place — see Rule 20-7.)

15-2 **Match Play**

If a player plays a stroke with a <u>wrong ball</u> except in a <u>hazard</u>, *he shall lose the hole.*

If a player plays any strokes in a hazard with a wrong ball, there is no penalty. Strokes played in a hazard with a wrong ball do not count in the player's score. If the wrong ball belongs to another player, its owner shall place a ball on the spot from which the wrong ball was first played.

If the player and opponent exchange balls during the play of a hole, the first to play the wrong ball other than from a hazard shall lose the hole; when this cannot be determined, the hole shall be played out with the balls exchanged.

15-3 **Stroke Play**

If a competitor plays a stroke or strokes with a <u>wrong ball</u>, *he shall incur a penalty of two strokes,* unless the only stroke or strokes played with such

---

ball were played when it was in a hazard, in which case no penalty is incurred.

The competitor must correct his mistake by playing the correct ball. If he fails to correct his mistake before he plays a stroke from the next <u>teeing ground</u> or, in the case of the last hole of the round, fails to declare his intention to correct his mistake before leaving the <u>putting green</u>, *he shall be disqualified.*

Strokes played by a competitor with a wrong ball do not count in his score.

If the wrong ball belongs to another competitor, its owner shall place a ball on the spot from which the wrong ball was first played.

(Lie of ball to be placed or replaced altered — see Rule 20-3b.)

The Putting Green

Rule 16 The Putting Green

Definitions

The "putting green" is all ground of the hole being played which is specially prepared for putting or otherwise defined as such by the Committee. A ball is on the putting green when any part of it touches the putting green.

The "line of putt" is the line which the player wishes his ball to take after a stroke on the <u>putting green</u>. Except with respect to Rule 16-1e, the line of putt includes a reasonable distance on either side of the intended line. The line of putt does not extend beyond the hole.

A ball is "holed" when it is at rest within the circumference of the hole and all of it is below the level of the lip of the hole.

16-1 General

a. TOUCHING LINE OF PUTT

The <u>line of putt</u> must not be touched except:
  (i) the player may move sand and loose soil on the putting green and other <u>loose impediments</u> by picking them up or by brushing them aside with his hand or a club without pressing anything down;
  (ii) in addressing the ball, the player may place the club in front of the ball without pressing anything down;
  (iii) in measuring — Rule 10-4;
  (iv) in lifting the ball — Rule 16-1b;
  (v) in pressing down a ball-marker;

  (vi) in repairing old hole plugs or ball marks
    on the putting green — Rule 16-1c; and
  (vii) in removing movable <u>obstructions</u> —
    Rule 24-1.

(Indicating line for putting on putting green —
see Rule 8-2b.)

b. LIFTING BALL

 A ball on the <u>putting green</u> may be lifted and,
if desired, cleaned. A ball so lifted shall be
replaced on the spot from which it was lifted.

c. REPAIR OF HOLE PLUGS, BALL MARKS AND
 OTHER DAMAGE

 The player may repair an old hole plug or damage to the <u>putting green</u> caused by the impact of a
ball, whether or not the player's ball lies on the
putting green. If the ball is moved in the process
of such repair, it shall be replaced, without
penalty. Any other damage to the putting green
shall not be repaired if it might assist the player in
his subsequent play of the hole.

d. TESTING SURFACE

 During the play of a hole, a player shall not
test the surface of the <u>putting green</u> by rolling a
ball or roughening or scraping the surface.

e. STANDING ASTRIDE OR ON LINE OF PUTT

 The player shall not make a <u>stroke</u> on the
<u>putting green</u> from a <u>stance</u> astride, or with
either foot touching, the line of putt or an extension of that line behind the ball.

f. POSITION OF CADDIE OR PARTNER

While making a <u>stroke</u> on the putting green, the player shall not allow his caddie, his partner or his partner's caddie to position himself on or close to an extension of the line of putt behind the ball.

g. PLAYING STROKE WHILE ANOTHER BALL IN MOTION

The player shall not play a stroke while another ball is in motion after a stroke from the putting green, except that, if a player does so, he incurs no penalty if it was his turn to play.

(Lifting ball interfering with or assisting play while another ball in motion — see Rule 22.)

PENALTY FOR BREACH OF RULE 16-1:
Match play — Loss of hole;
Stroke play — Two strokes.

16-2 **Ball Overhanging Hole**

When any part of the ball overhangs the lip of the hole, the player is allowed enough time to reach the hole without unreasonable delay and an additional ten seconds to determine whether the ball is at rest. If by then the ball has not fallen into the hole, it is deemed to be at rest. If the ball subsequently falls into the hole, the player is deemed to have holed out with his last stroke, and *he shall add a penalty stroke to his score* for the hole; otherwise there is no penalty under this Rule.

(Undue delay — see Rule 6-7.)

Rule 17 The Flagstick

17-1 Flagstick Attended, Removed or Held Up

Before and during the <u>stroke</u>, the player may have the flagstick attended, removed or held up to indicate the position of the hole. This may be done only on the authority of the player before he plays his stroke.

If, prior to the stroke, the flagstick is attended, removed or held up by anyone with the player's knowledge and no objection is made, the player shall be deemed to have authorized it. If anyone attends or holds up the flagstick or stands near the hole while a stroke is being played, he shall be deemed to be attending the flagstick until the ball comes to rest.

17-2 Unauthorized Attendance

a. MATCH PLAY

In match play, an opponent or his caddie shall not, without the authority or prior knowledge of the player, attend, remove or hold up the flagstick while the player is making a stroke or his ball is in motion.

b. STROKE PLAY

In stroke play, if a fellow-competitor or his caddie attends, removes or holds up the flagstick without the competitor's authority or prior knowledge while the competitor is making a stroke or his ball is in motion, *the fellow-competitor shall incur the penalty* for breach of this Rule. In such circumstances, if the competitor's ball strikes the flagstick, the person attending it or anything carried by him, the competitor incurs no penalty and the ball shall be played as it lies, except that, if the stroke was played from the putting green, the stroke shall be cancelled, the ball replaced and the stroke replayed.

PENALTY FOR BREACH OF RULE 17-1 OR -2:
Match play — Loss of hole;
Stroke play — Two strokes.

17-3 **Ball Striking Flagstick or Attendant**
The player's ball shall not strike:

a. The flagstick when attended, removed or held up by the player, his partner or either of their caddies, or by another person with the player's authority or prior knowledge; or

b. The player's caddie, his partner or his partner's caddie when attending the flagstick, or another person attending the flagstick with the player's authority or prior knowledge or anything carried by any such person; or

c. The flagstick in the hole, unattended, when the ball has been played from the putting green.

PENALTY FOR BREACH OF RULE 17-3:
Match play — Loss of hole;
Stroke play — Two strokes and the ball
shall be played as it lies.

17-4 **Ball Resting Against Flagstick**
If the ball rests against the flagstick when it is in the hole, the player or another person authorized by him may move or remove the flagstick and if the ball falls into the hole, the player shall be deemed to have holed out with his last stroke; otherwise, the ball, if <u>moved</u>, shall be placed on the lip of the hole, without penalty.

Ball Moved, Deflected or Stopped

Rule 18   **Ball at Rest Moved**

Definitions

A ball is deemed to have "moved" if it leaves its position and comes to rest in any other place.

An "outside agency" is any agency not part of the match or, in stroke play, not part of the competitor's side, and includes a referee, a marker, an observer and a forecaddie. Neither wind nor water is an outside agency.

"Equipment" is anything used, worn or carried by or for the player except any ball he has played at the hole being played and any small object, such as a coin or a tee, when used to mark the position of a ball or the extent of an area in which a ball is to be dropped. Equipment includes a golf cart, whether or not motorized. If such a cart is shared by two or more players, the cart and everything in it are deemed to be the equipment of the player whose ball is involved except that, when the cart is being moved by one of the players sharing it, the cart and everything in it are deemed to be that player's equipment.

Note: A ball played at the hole being played is equipment when it has been lifted and not put back into play.

A player has "addressed the ball" when he has taken his <u>stance</u> and has also grounded his club, except that in a <u>hazard</u> a player has addressed the ball when he has taken his stance.

Taking the "stance" consists in a player placing

his feet in position for and preparatory to making a
<u>stroke</u>.

18-1 By Outside Agency

If a ball at rest is moved by an <u>outside agency</u>,
the player shall incur no penalty and the ball shall
be replaced before the player plays another <u>stroke</u>.

(Player's ball at rest moved by another ball —
see Rule 18-5.)

18-2 By Player, Partner, Caddie or Equipment

a. GENERAL

When a player's ball is <u>in play</u>, if:

(i)   the player, his partner or either of their
      caddies lifts or moves it, touches it pur-
      posely (except with a club in the act of
      addressing it) or causes it to move except
      as permitted by a Rule, or

(ii) equipment of the player or his partner
      causes the ball to move,

the player shall incur a penalty stroke. The ball
shall be replaced unless the movement of the ball
occurs after the player has begun his swing and
he does not discontinue his swing.

Under the Rules no penalty is incurred if a
player accidentally causes his ball to move in the
following circumstances:

In measuring to determine which ball farther
    from hole — Rule 10-4

In searching for covered ball in <u>hazard</u> or for
    ball in <u>casual water, ground under repair,</u>
    etc. — Rule 12-1

In the process of repairing hole plug or ball
  mark — Rule 16-1c

In the process of removing <u>loose impediment</u>
  on <u>putting green</u> — Rule 18-2c

In the process of lifting ball under a Rule —
  Rule 20-1

In the process of placing or replacing ball
  under a Rule — Rule 20-3a

In removal of movable <u>obstruction</u> — Rule
  24-1.

b. BALL MOVING AFTER ADDRESS

If a player's <u>ball in play moves</u> after he has
<u>addressed</u> it (other than as a result of a stroke),
the player shall be deemed to have moved the
ball and *shall incur a penalty stroke.* The player
shall replace the ball unless the movement of the
ball occurs after he has begun his swing and he
does not discontinue his swing.

c. BALL MOVING AFTER LOOSE IMPEDIMENT
  TOUCHED

<u>Through the green</u>, if the ball <u>moves</u> after any
<u>loose impediment</u> lying within a club-length of
it has been touched by the player, his partner or
either of their caddies and before the player has
<u>addressed</u> it, the player shall be deemed to have
moved the ball and *shall incur a penalty stroke.*
The player shall replace the ball unless the movement of the ball occurs after he has begun his
swing and he does not discontinue his swing.

On the <u>putting green</u>, if the ball or the ball-
marker <u>moves</u> in the process of removing any
<u>loose impediment</u>, the ball or the ball-marker

shall be replaced. There is no penalty provided the movement of the ball or the ball-marker is directly attributable to the removal of the loose impediment. Otherwise, *the player shall incur a penalty stroke* under Rule 18-2a or 20-1.

18-3 By Opponent, Caddie or Equipment in Match Play

a. During Search

If, during search for a player's ball, the ball is moved by an opponent, his caddie or his <u>equipment</u>, no penalty is incurred and the player shall replace the ball.

b. Other than During Search

If, other than during search for a ball, the ball is touched or moved by an opponent, his caddie or his <u>equipment</u>, except as otherwise provided in the Rules, *the opponent shall incur a penalty stroke*. The player shall replace the ball.

(Ball moved in measuring to determine which ball farther from the hole — see Rule 10-4.)

(Playing a wrong ball — see Rule 15-2.)

18-4 By Fellow-Competitor, Caddie or Equipment in Stroke Play

If a competitor's ball is moved by a fellow-competitor, his caddie or his <u>equipment</u>, no penalty is incurred. The competitor shall replace his ball.

(Playing a wrong ball — see Rule 15-3.)

18-5 By Another Ball

If a ball in play and at rest is moved by another ball in motion after a stroke, the moved ball shall be replaced.

*PENALTY FOR BREACH OF RULE:
Match play — Loss of hole;
Stroke play — Two strokes.
*If a player who is required to replace a ball fails
to do so, he shall incur the general penalty
for breach of Rule 18 but no additional penalty
under Rule 18 shall be applied.

Note 1: If a ball to be replaced under this Rule is not immediately recoverable, another ball may be substituted.

Note 2: If it is impossible to determine the spot on which a ball is to be placed, see Rule 20-3c.

Rule 19 Ball in Motion Deflected or Stopped

Definitions

An "outside agency" is any agency not part of the match or, in stroke play, not part of the competitor's side, and includes a referee, a marker, an observer and a forecaddie. Neither wind nor water is an outside agency.

"Equipment" is anything used, worn or carried by or for the player except any ball he has played at the hole being played and any small object, such as a coin or a tee, when used to mark the position of a ball or the extent of an area in which a ball is to be dropped. Equipment includes a golf cart, whether or not motorized. If such a cart is shared by two or more players, the cart and everything in it are deemed to be the equipment of the player whose ball is involved except that, when the cart is being moved by one of the players sharing it, the cart and everything in it are deemed to be that player's equipment.

Note: A ball played at the hole being played is
equipment when it has been lifted and not put
back into play.

19-1 **By Outside Agency**

If a ball in motion is accidentally deflected or
stopped by any <u>outside agency</u>, it is a <u>rub of the
green</u>, no penalty is incurred and the ball shall be
played as it lies except:

a. If a ball in motion after a <u>stroke</u> other than on the
<u>putting green</u> comes to rest in or on any moving
or animate outside agency, the player shall,
<u>through the green</u> or in a <u>hazard</u>, drop the ball, or
on the putting green place the ball, as near as possible to the spot where the outside agency was
when the ball came to rest in or on it, and

b. If a ball in motion after a stroke on the putting
green is deflected or stopped by, or comes to rest
in or on, any moving or animate outside agency
except a worm or an insect, the stroke shall be
cancelled, the ball replaced and the stroke
replayed.

If the ball is not immediately recoverable,
another ball may be substituted.

(Player's ball deflected or stopped by another
ball — see Rule 19-5.)

Note: If the referee or the Committee determines
that a player's ball has been purposely deflected or
stopped by an <u>outside agency</u>, Rule 1-4 applies to
the player. If the outside agency is a fellow-competitor or his caddie, Rule 1-2 applies to the fellow-competitor.

19-2 **By Player, Partner, Caddie or Equipment**

a. MATCH PLAY

If a player's ball is accidentally deflected or stopped by himself, his partner or either of their caddies or <u>equipment</u>, *he shall lose the hole.*

b. STROKE PLAY

If a competitor's ball is accidentally deflected or stopped by himself, his partner or either of their caddies or <u>equipment</u>, *the competitor shall incur a penalty of two strokes.* The ball shall be played as it lies, except when it comes to rest in or on the competitor's, his partner's or either of their caddies' clothes or equipment, in which case the competitor shall <u>through the green</u> or in a <u>hazard</u> drop the ball, or on the <u>putting green</u> place the ball, as near as possible to where the article was when the ball came to rest in or on it.

Exception: Dropped ball — see Rule 20-2a.

(Ball purposely deflected or stopped by player, partner or caddie — see Rule 1-2.)

19-3 **By Opponent, Caddie or Equipment in Match Play**

If a player's ball is accidentally deflected or stopped by an opponent, his caddie or his <u>equipment</u>, no penalty is incurred. The player may play the ball as it lies or, before another <u>stroke</u> is played by either side, cancel the stroke and play a ball without penalty as nearly as possible at the spot from which the original ball was last played (see Rule 20-5).

If the ball has come to rest in or on the opponent's or his caddie's clothes or equipment, the player may <u>through the green</u> or in a <u>hazard</u> drop the ball, or on the putting green place the ball, as

near as possible to where the article was when the
ball came to rest in or on it.

Exception: Ball striking person attending flagstick — see Rule 17-3b.

(Ball purposely deflected or stopped by opponent or caddie — see Rule 1-2.)

19-4 **By Fellow-Competitor, Caddie or Equipment
in Stroke Play**

See Rule 19-1 regarding ball deflected by outside
agency.

19-5 **By Another Ball**

a. AT REST

If a player's ball in motion after a stroke is
deflected or stopped by a ball in play and at rest,
the player shall play his ball as it lies. In match
play, no penalty is incurred. In stroke play, there
is no penalty unless both balls lay on the <u>putting
green</u> prior to the stroke, in which case *the player
incurs a penalty of two strokes.*

b. IN MOTION

If a player's ball in motion after a stroke is
deflected or stopped by another ball in motion
after a stroke, the player shall play his ball as it
lies. There is no penalty unless the player was in
breach of Rule 16-1g, in which case *he shall
incur the penalty for breach of that Rule.*

Exception: If the player's ball is in motion after
a stroke on the putting green and the other ball in
motion is an outside agency — see Rule 19-1b.

PENALTY FOR BREACH OF RULE:
Match play — Loss of hole;
Stroke play — Two strokes.

Relief Situations and Procedure

| Rule 20 | **Lifting, Dropping and Placing; Playing from Wrong Place** |

20-1 **Lifting**

A ball to be lifted under the Rules may be lifted by the player, his partner or another person authorized by the player. In any such case, the player shall be responsible for any breach of the Rules.

The position of the ball shall be marked before it is lifted under a Rule which requires it to be replaced. If it is not marked, *the player shall incur a penalty of one stroke* and the ball shall be replaced. If it is not replaced, *the player shall incur the general penalty* for breach of this Rule but no additional penalty under Rule 20-1 shall be applied.

If a ball or ball-marker is accidentally moved in the process of lifting the ball under a Rule or marking its position, the ball or the ball-marker shall be replaced. There is no penalty provided the movement of the ball or the ball-marker is directly attributable to the specific act of marking the position of or lifting the ball. Otherwise, *the player shall incur a penalty stroke* under this Rule or Rule 18-2a.

Exception: If a player incurs a penalty for failing to act in accordance with Rule 5-3 or 12-2, no additional penalty under Rule 20-1 shall be applied.

Note: The position of a ball to be lifted should be marked by placing a ball-marker, a small coin or other similar object immediately behind the ball. If the ball-marker interferes with the play, <u>stance</u> or <u>stroke</u> of another player, it should be placed one or more clubhead-lengths to one side.

20-2 **Dropping and Re-dropping**

a. BY WHOM AND HOW

A ball to be dropped under the Rules shall be dropped by the player himself. He shall stand erect, hold the ball at shoulder height and arm's length and drop it. If a ball is dropped by any other person or in any other manner and the error is not corrected as provided in Rule 20-6, *the player shall incur a penalty stroke.*

If the ball touches the player, his partner, either of their caddies or their equipment before or after it strikes a part of the course, the ball shall be re-dropped, without penalty. There is no limit to the number of times a ball shall be re-dropped in such circumstances.

(Taking action to influence position or movement of ball — see Rule 1-2.)

b. WHERE TO DROP

When a ball is to be dropped as near as possible to a specific spot, it shall be dropped not nearer the hole than the specific spot which, if it is not precisely known to the player, shall be estimated.

A ball when dropped must first strike a part of the course where the applicable Rule requires it to be dropped. If it is not so dropped, Rules 20-6 and -7 apply.

c. WHEN TO RE-DROP

A dropped ball shall be re-dropped without penalty if it:

(i) rolls into a <u>hazard</u>;

    (ii) rolls out of a hazard;

    (iii) rolls onto a <u>putting green</u>;

    (iv) rolls <u>out of bounds</u>;

    (v) rolls to a position where there is interference by the condition from which relief was taken under Rule 24-2 (immovable obstruction) or Rule 25-1 (abnormal ground conditions), or rolls back into the pitch-mark from which it was lifted under Rule 25-2 (embedded ball);

    (vi) rolls and comes to rest more than two club-lengths from where it first struck a part of the course;

    (vii) rolls and comes to rest nearer the hole than its original position or estimated position (see Rule 20-2b) unless otherwise permitted by the Rules; or

    (viii) rolls and comes to rest nearer the hole than the point where the original ball last crossed the margin of the area or hazard, (Rule 25-1c(i) and (ii)) or the margin of the water hazard (Rule 26-1b) or lateral water hazard (Rule 26-1c).

If the ball when re-dropped rolls into any position listed above, it shall be placed as near as possible to the spot where it first struck a part of the course when re-dropped.

If a ball to be re-dropped or placed under this Rule is not immediately recoverable, another ball may be substituted.

20-3 **Placing and Replacing**

a. By Whom and Where

A ball to be placed under the Rules shall be placed by the player or his partner. If a ball is to be replaced, the player, his partner or the person who lifted or moved it shall place it on the spot from which it was lifted or moved. In any such case, the player shall be responsible for any breach of the Rules.

If a ball or ball-marker is accidentally moved in the process of placing or replacing the ball, the ball or the ball-marker shall be replaced. There is no penalty provided the movement of the ball or the ball-marker is directly attributable to the specific act of placing or replacing the ball or removing the ball-marker. Otherwise, *the player shall incur a penalty stroke* under Rule 18-2a or 20-1.

b. Lie of Ball to be Placed
or Replaced Altered

If the original lie of a ball to be placed or replaced has been altered:

(i) except in a <u>hazard</u>, the ball shall be placed in the nearest lie most similar to the original lie which is not more than one club-length from the original lie, not nearer the hole and not in a hazard;

(ii) in a <u>water hazard</u>, the ball shall be placed in accordance with Clause (i) above, except that the ball must be placed in the water hazard;

(iii) in a <u>bunker</u>, the original lie shall be re-

created as nearly as possible and the ball
shall be placed in that lie.

c. Spot Not Determinable

If it is impossible to determine the spot where
the ball is to be placed or replaced:

(i)   <u>through the green</u>, the ball shall be
       dropped as near as possible to the place
       where it lay but not in a hazard or on a
       putting green;

(ii) in a hazard, the ball shall be dropped in
       the hazard as near as possible to the place
       where it lay;

(iii) on the <u>putting green</u>, the ball shall be
       placed as near as possible to the place
       where it lay but not in a hazard.

d. Ball Fails to Come to Rest on Spot

If a ball when placed fails to come to rest on
the spot on which it was placed, it shall be
replaced without penalty. If it still fails to come
to rest on that spot:

(i)   except in a <u>hazard</u>, it shall be placed at
       the nearest spot not nearer the hole or in
       a hazard where it can be placed at rest;

(ii) in a hazard, it shall be placed in the haz-
       ard at the nearest spot not nearer the hole
       where it can be placed at rest.

If a ball when placed comes to rest on the spot
on which it is placed, and it subsequently moves,
there is no penalty and the ball shall be played as it
lies, unless the provisions of any other Rule apply.

PENALTY FOR BREACH OF RULE 20-1, -2 OR -3:
Match play — Loss of hole;
Stroke play — Two strokes.

20-4 **When Ball Dropped or Placed Is in Play**

If the player's <u>ball in play</u> has been lifted, it is again in play when dropped or placed.

A substituted ball becomes the ball in play when it has been dropped or placed.

(Ball incorrectly substituted — see Rule 15-1.)

(Lifting ball incorrectly substituted, dropped or placed — see Rule 20-6.)

20-5 **Playing Next Stroke from Where Previous Stroke Played**

When, under the Rules, a player elects or is required to play his next <u>stroke</u> from where a previous stroke was played, he shall proceed as follows: If the stroke is to be played from the <u>teeing ground</u>, the ball to be played shall be played from anywhere within the teeing ground and may be teed; if the stroke is to be played from <u>through the green</u> or a <u>hazard</u>, it shall be dropped; if the stroke is to be played on the <u>putting green</u>, it shall be placed.

PENALTY FOR BREACH OF RULE 20-5:
Match play — Loss of hole;
Stroke play — Two strokes.

20-6 **Lifting Ball Incorrectly Substituted, Dropped or Placed**

A ball incorrectly substituted, dropped or placed in a wrong place or otherwise not in accordance with the Rules but not played may be lifted, without penalty, and the player shall then proceed correctly.

20-7 **Playing from Wrong Place**

For a ball played from outside the teeing ground or from a wrong teeing ground — see Rule 11-4 and -5.

a. MATCH PLAY

If a player plays a stroke with a ball which has been dropped or placed in a wrong place, *he shall lose the hole.*

b. STROKE PLAY

If a competitor plays a stroke with his <u>ball in play</u> (i) which has been dropped or placed in a wrong place or (ii) which has been moved and not replaced in a case where the Rules require replacement, *he shall*, provided a serious breach has not occurred, *incur the penalty prescribed by the applicable Rule* and play out the hole with the ball.

If, after playing from a wrong place, a competitor becomes aware of that fact and believes that a serious breach may be involved, he may, provided he has not played a stroke from the next teeing ground or, in the case of the last hole of the round, left the putting green, declare that he will play out the hole with a second ball dropped or placed in accordance with the Rules. The competitor shall report the facts to the Committee before returning his score card; if he fails to do so, *he shall be disqualified.* The Committee shall determine whether a serious breach of the Rule occurred. If so, the score with the second ball shall count and *the competitor shall add two penalty strokes to his score with that ball.*

If a serious breach has occurred and the competitor has failed to correct it as prescribed above, *he shall be disqualified.*

Note: If a competitor plays a second ball, penalty strokes incurred by playing the ball ruled not to count and strokes subsequently taken with that ball shall be disregarded.

Rule 21 Cleaning Ball

A ball on the putting green may be cleaned when lifted under Rule 16-1b. Elsewhere, a ball may be cleaned when lifted except when it has been lifted:

a. To determine if it is unfit for play (Rule 5-3);

b. For identification (Rule 12-2), in which case it may be cleaned only to the extent necessary for identification; or

c. Because it is interfering with or assisting play (Rule 22).

If a player cleans his ball during play of a hole except as provided in this Rule, *he shall incur a penalty of one stroke* and the ball, if lifted, shall be replaced.

If a player who is required to replace a ball fails to do so, *he shall incur the penalty* for breach of Rule 20-3a, but no additional penalty under Rule 21 shall be applied.

Exception: If a player incurs a penalty for failing to act in accordance with Rule 5-3, 12-2 or 22, no additional penalty under Rule 21 shall be applied.

Rule 22 **Ball Interfering with or Assisting Play**

Any player may:

a. Lift his ball if he considers that the ball might assist any other player or

b. Have any other ball lifted if he considers that the ball might interfere with his play or assist the play of any other player,

but this may not be done while another ball is in motion. In stroke play, a player required to lift his ball may play first rather than lift. A ball lifted under this Rule shall be replaced.

> **PENALTY FOR BREACH OF RULE:**
> *Match play — Loss of hole;*
> *Stroke play — Two strokes.*

Note: Except on the putting green, the ball may not be cleaned when lifted under this Rule — see Rule 21.

Rule 23 **Loose Impediments**

Definition

"Loose impediments" are natural objects such as stones, leaves, twigs, branches and the like, dung, worms and insects and casts or heaps made by them, provided they are not fixed or growing, are not solidly embedded and do not adhere to the ball.

Sand and loose soil are loose impediments on the <u>putting green</u> but not elsewhere.

Snow and natural ice, other than frost, are either <u>casual water</u> or loose impediments, at the option of the player. Manufactured ice is an <u>obstruction</u>.

Dew and frost are not loose impediments.

23-1 **Relief**

Except when both the <u>loose impediment</u> and the ball lie in or touch the same <u>hazard</u>, any loose impediment may be removed without penalty. If the ball moves, see Rule 18-2c.

When a ball is in motion, a loose impediment which might influence the movement of the ball shall not be removed.

PENALTY FOR BREACH OF RULE:
Match play — Loss of hole;
Stroke play — Two strokes.
(Searching for ball in hazard — see Rule 12-1.)
(Touching line of putt — see Rule 16-1a.)

Rule 24 **Obstructions**

Definition

An "obstruction" is anything artificial, including the artificial surfaces and sides of roads and paths and manufactured ice, except:

a. Objects defining <u>out of bounds</u>, such as walls, fences, stakes and railings;

b. Any part of an immovable artificial object which is out of bounds; and

c. Any construction declared by the Committee to be an integral part of the course.

24-1 **Movable Obstruction**

A player may obtain relief from a movable <u>obstruction</u> as follows:

a. If the ball does not lie in or on the obstruction, the obstruction may be removed. If the ball moves, it shall be replaced, and there is no

---

penalty provided that the movement of the ball is directly attributable to the removal of the obstruction. Otherwise, Rule 18-2a applies.

b. If the ball lies in or on the obstruction, the ball may be lifted, without penalty, and the obstruction removed. The ball shall <u>through the green</u> or in a <u>hazard</u> be dropped, or on the <u>putting green</u> be placed, as near as possible to the spot directly under the place where the ball lay in or on the obstruction, but not nearer the hole.

The ball may be cleaned when lifted under Rule 24-1.

When a ball is in motion, an obstruction which might influence the movement of the ball, other than an attended flagstick or equipment of the players, shall not be removed.

Note: If a ball to be dropped or placed under this Rule is not immediately recoverable, another ball may be substituted.

24-2 **Immovable Obstruction**

a. INTERFERENCE

Interference by an immovable <u>obstruction</u> occurs when a ball lies in or on the obstruction, or so close to the obstruction that the obstruction interferes with the player's <u>stance</u> or the area of his intended swing. If the player's ball lies on the <u>putting green</u>, interference also occurs if an immovable obstruction on the putting green intervenes on his line of putt. Otherwise, intervention on the line of play is not, of itself, interference under this Rule.

b. RELIEF

Except when the ball is in a <u>water hazard</u> or a <u>lateral water hazard</u>, a player may obtain relief from interference by an immovable <u>obstruction</u>, without penalty, as follows:

(i) *Through the Green:* If the ball lies <u>through the green</u>, the point on the <u>course</u> nearest to where the ball lies shall be determined (without crossing over, through or under the obstruction) which (a) is not nearer the hole, (b) avoids interference (as defined) and (c) is not in a <u>hazard</u> or on a <u>putting green</u>. The player shall lift the ball and drop it within one club-length of the point thus determined on a part of the course which fulfills (a), (b) and (c) above.

Note: The prohibition against crossing over, through or under the <u>obstruction</u> does not apply to the artificial surfaces and sides of roads and paths or when the ball lies in or on the obstruction.

(ii) *In a Bunker:* If the ball is in a <u>bunker</u>, the player shall lift and drop the ball in accordance with Clause (i) above, except that the ball must be dropped in the bunker.

(iii) *On the Putting Green:* If the ball lies on the <u>putting green</u>, the player shall lift the ball and place it in the nearest position to where it lay which affords relief from interference, but not nearer the hole nor in a hazard.

The ball may be cleaned when lifted under Rule 24-2b.

(Ball rolling to a position where there is interference by the condition from which relief was taken — see Rule 20-2c(v).)

Exception: A player may not obtain relief under Rule 24-2b if (a) it is clearly unreasonable for him to play a stroke because of interference by anything other than an immovable obstruction or (b) interference by an immovable obstruction would occur only through use of an unnecessarily abnormal stance, swing or direction of play.

Note 1: If a ball is in a water hazard (including a lateral water hazard), the player is not entitled to relief without penalty from interference by an immovable obstruction. The player shall play the ball as it lies or proceed under Rule 26-1.

Note 2: If a ball to be dropped or placed under this Rule is not immediately recoverable, another ball may be substituted.

c. BALL LOST

Except in a water hazard or a lateral water hazard, if there is reasonable evidence that a ball is lost in an immovable obstruction, the player may, without penalty, substitute another ball and follow the procedure prescribed in Rule 24-2b. For the purpose of applying this Rule, the ball shall be deemed to lie at the spot where it entered the obstruction. If the ball is lost in an underground drain pipe or culvert the entrance to which is in a hazard, a ball must be dropped in that hazard or the player may proceed under Rule 26-1, if applicable.

PENALTY FOR BREACH OF RULE:
Match play — Loss of hole;
Stroke play — Two strokes.

Rule 25 **Abnormal Ground Conditions**
and Wrong Putting Green

Definitions

"Casual water" is any temporary accumulation of water on the <u>course</u> which is visible before or after the player takes his <u>stance</u> and is not in a <u>water hazard</u>. Snow and natural ice, other than frost, are casual water or <u>loose impediments</u>, at the option of the player. Manufactured ice is an <u>obstruction</u>. Dew and frost are not casual water. A ball is in casual water when it lies in or any part of it touches the casual water.

"Ground under repair" is any portion of the <u>course</u> so marked by order of the Committee or so declared by its authorized representative. It includes material piled for removal and a hole made by a greenkeeper, even if not so marked. Stakes and lines defining ground under repair are in such ground. Stakes defining ground under repair are obstructions. The margin of ground under repair extends vertically downwards, but not upwards. A ball is in ground under repair when it lies in or any part of it touches the ground under repair.

Note 1: Grass cuttings and other material left on the course which have been abandoned and are not intended to be removed are not ground under repair unless so marked.

Note 2: The Committee may make a Local Rule prohibiting play from ground under repair or an environmentally-sensitive area which has been defined as ground under repair.

25-1 Casual Water, Ground Under Repair and Certain Damage to Course

a. INTERFERENCE

Interference by <u>casual water</u>, <u>ground under repair</u> or a hole, cast or runway made by a burrowing animal, a reptile or a bird occurs when a ball lies in or touches any of these conditions or when such a condition on the <u>course</u> interferes with the player's <u>stance</u> or the area of his intended swing.

If the player's ball lies on the <u>putting green</u>, interference also occurs if such condition on the putting green intervenes on his line of putt.

If interference exists, the player may either play the ball as it lies (unless prohibited by Local Rule) or take relief as provided in Clause b.

Note: The Committee may make a Local Rule denying the player relief from interference with his stance by all or any of the conditions covered by this Rule.

b. RELIEF

If the player elects to take relief, he shall proceed as follows:

(i) *Through the Green:* If the ball lies <u>through the green</u>, the point on the <u>course</u> nearest to where the ball lies shall be determined which (a) is not nearer the hole, (b) avoids interference by the condition, and (c) is not in a <u>hazard</u> or on a <u>putting green</u>. The player shall lift the ball and drop it without penalty within one club-length of the point thus determined on a part of the course which fulfills (a), (b) and (c) above.

(ii) *In a Hazard:* If the ball is in a <u>hazard</u>, the player shall lift and drop the ball either:

    (a) Without penalty, in the hazard, as near as possible to the spot where the ball lay, but not nearer the hole, on a part of the course which affords maximum available relief from the condition;

        or

    (b) *Under penalty of one stroke,* outside the hazard, keeping the point where the ball lay directly between the hole and the spot on which the ball is dropped, with no limit to how far behind the hazard the ball may be dropped.

    Exception: If a ball is in a <u>water hazard</u> (including a <u>lateral water hazard</u>), the player is not entitled to relief without penalty from a hole, cast or runway made by a burrowing animal, a reptile or a bird. The player shall play the ball as it lies or proceed under Rule 26-1.

(iii) *On the Putting Green:* If the ball lies on the <u>putting green</u>, the player shall lift the ball and place it without penalty in the nearest position to where it lay which affords maximum available relief from the condition, but not nearer the hole nor in a <u>hazard</u>.

The ball may be cleaned when lifted under Rule 25-1b.

(Ball rolling to a position where there is interference by the condition from which relief was taken — see Rule 20-2c(v).)

Exception: A player may not obtain relief under Rule 25-1b if (a) it is clearly unreasonable for him to play a stroke because of interference by anything other than a condition covered by Rule 25-1a or (b) interference by such a condition would occur only through use of an unnecessarily abnormal stance, swing or direction of play.

Note: If a ball to be dropped or placed under this Rule is not immediately recoverable, another ball may be substituted.

c. BALL LOST UNDER CONDITION
COVERED BY RULE 25-1

It is a question of fact whether a ball lost after having been struck toward a condition covered by Rule 25-1 is lost under such condition. In order to treat the ball as lost under such condition, there must be reasonable evidence to that effect. In the absence of such evidence, the ball must be treated as a lost ball and Rule 27 applies.

(i) *Outside a Hazard* — If a ball is lost outside a <u>hazard</u> under a condition covered by Rule 25-1, the player may take relief as follows: the point on the <u>course</u> nearest to where the ball last crossed the margin of the area shall be determined which (a) is not nearer the hole than where the ball last crossed the margin, (b) avoids interference by the condition and (c) is not in a hazard or on a <u>putting green</u>. He shall drop a ball without penalty within one club-length of the point thus determined on a part of the course which fulfills (a), (b) and (c) above.

(ii) *In a Hazard* — If a ball is lost in a <u>hazard</u> under a condition covered by Rule 25-1, the player may drop a ball either:

(a) Without penalty, in the hazard, as near as possible to the point at which the original ball last crossed the margin of the area, but not nearer the hole, on a part of the course which affords maximum available relief from the condition

   or

(b) *Under penalty of one stroke*, outside the hazard, keeping the point at which the original ball last crossed the margin of the hazard directly between the hole and the spot on which the ball is dropped, with no limit to how far behind the hazard the ball may be dropped.

Exception: If a ball is in a <u>water hazard</u> (including a <u>lateral water hazard</u>), the player is not entitled to relief without penalty for a ball lost in a hole, cast or runway made by a burrowing animal, a reptile or a bird. The player shall proceed under Rule 26-1.

25-2   Embedded Ball

A ball embedded in its own pitch-mark in the ground in any closely mown area <u>through the green</u> may be lifted, cleaned and dropped, without penalty, as near as possible to the spot where it lay but not nearer the hole. The ball when dropped must first strike a part of the course through the green. "Closely mown area" means any area of the <u>course</u>, including paths through the rough, cut to fairway height or less.

25-3   Wrong Putting Green

A player must not play a ball which lies on a <u>putting green</u> other than that of the hole being played. The ball must be lifted and the player must proceed as follows: The point on the course nearest to where the ball lies shall be determined which (a) is not nearer the hole and (b) is not in a <u>hazard</u> or on a putting green. The player shall lift the ball and drop it without penalty within one club-length of the point thus determined on a part of the course which fulfills (a) and (b) above. The ball may be cleaned when so lifted.

Note: Unless otherwise prescribed by the Committee, the term "a putting green other than that of the hole being played" includes a practice putting green or pitching green on the course.

PENALTY FOR BREACH OF RULE:
Match play — Loss of hole;
Stroke play — Two strokes.

Rule 26 Water Hazards (Including Lateral Water Hazards)

Definitions

A "water hazard" is any sea, lake, pond, river, ditch, surface drainage ditch or other open water course (whether or not containing water) and anything of a similar nature.

All ground or water within the margin of a water hazard is part of the water hazard. The margin of a water hazard extends vertically upwards and downwards. Stakes and lines defining the margins of water hazards are in the hazards. Such stakes are <u>obstructions</u>. A ball is in a water hazard when it lies in or any part of it touches the water hazard.

Note 1: Water hazards (other than <u>lateral water hazards</u>) should be defined by yellow stakes or lines.

Note 2: The Committee may make a Local Rule prohibiting play from an environmentally-sensitive area which has been defined as a water hazard.

A "lateral water hazard" is a <u>water hazard</u> or that part of a water hazard so situated that it is not possible or is deemed by the Committee to be impracticable to drop a ball behind the water hazard in accordance with Rule 26-1b.

That part of a water hazard to be played as a lateral water hazard should be distinctively marked. A ball is in a lateral water hazard when it lies in or any part of it touches the lateral water hazard.

Note 1: Lateral water hazards should be defined by red stakes or lines.

Note 2: The Committee may make a Local Rule prohibiting play from an environmentally-sensitive area which has been defined as a lateral water hazard.

26-1 **Ball in Water Hazard**

It is a question of fact whether a ball lost after having been struck toward a <u>water hazard</u> is lost inside or outside the hazard. In order to treat the ball as lost in the hazard, there must be reasonable evidence that the ball lodged in it. In the absence of such evidence, the ball must be treated as a lost ball and Rule 27 applies.

If a ball is in or is lost in a water hazard (whether the ball lies in water or not), the player may *under penalty of one stroke*:

a. Play a ball as nearly as possible at the spot from which the original ball was last played (see Rule 20-5);
   or

b. Drop a ball behind the water hazard, keeping the point at which the original ball last crossed the margin of the water hazard directly between the hole and the spot on which the ball is dropped, with no limit to how far behind the water hazard the ball may be dropped;
   or

c. *As additional options available only if the ball last crossed the margin of a lateral water hazard*, drop a ball outside the water hazard within two club-lengths of and not nearer the hole than (i) the point where the original ball last crossed the margin of the water hazard or (ii) a point on the opposite margin of the water hazard equidistant from the hole.

The ball may be cleaned when lifted under this Rule.

(Ball moving in water in a water hazard — see Rule 14-6.)

26-2 Ball Played Within Water Hazard

a. BALL COMES TO REST IN THE HAZARD

If a ball played from within a water hazard comes to rest in the same hazard after the stroke, the player may:

  (i) proceed under Rule 26-1; or
  (ii) *under penalty of one stroke*, play a ball as nearly as possible at the spot from which the last stroke from outside the hazard was played (see Rule 20-5).

If the player proceeds under Rule 26-1a, he may elect not to play the dropped ball. If he so elects, he may:

  a. Proceed under Rule 26-1b, *adding the additional penalty of one stroke* prescribed by that Rule;
     or

  b. Proceed under Rule 26-1c, if applicable, *adding the additional penalty of one stroke* prescribed by that Rule;
     or

  c. *Add an additional penalty of one stroke* and play a ball as nearly as possible at the spot from which the last stroke from outside the hazard was played (see Rule 20-5).

b. BALL LOST OR UNPLAYABLE OUTSIDE HAZARD
   OR OUT OF BOUNDS

If a ball played from within a water hazard is lost or declared unplayable outside the hazard or is out of bounds, the player, after taking *a penalty of one stroke* under Rule 27-1 or 28a, may:

(i)   play a ball as nearly as possible at the spot in the hazard from which the original ball was last played (see Rule 20-5); or

(ii) proceed under Rule 26-1b, or if applicable Rule 26-1c, *adding the additional penalty of one stroke* prescribed by the Rule and using as the reference point the point where the original ball last crossed the margin of the hazard before it came to rest in the hazard; or

(iii) *add an additional penalty of one stroke* and play a ball as nearly as possible at the spot from which the last stroke from outside the hazard was played (see Rule 20-5).

Note 1: When proceeding under Rule 26-2b, the player is not required to drop a ball under Rule 27-1 or 28a. If he does drop a ball, he is not required to play it. He may alternatively proceed under Clause (ii) or (iii).

Note 2: If a ball played from within a water hazard is declared unplayable outside the hazard, nothing in Rule 26-2b precludes the player from proceeding under Rule 28b or c.

PENALTY FOR BREACH OF RULE:
Match play — Loss of hole;
Stroke play — Two strokes.

Rule 27   **Ball Lost or Out of Bounds; Provisional Ball**

If the original ball is lost in an immovable obstruction (Rule 24-2) or under a condition covered by Rule 25-1 (casual water, ground under repair and certain damage to the course), the player may proceed under the applicable Rule. If the original ball is lost in a water hazard, the player shall proceed under Rule 26.

Such Rules may not be used unless there is reasonable evidence that the ball is lost in an immovable obstruction, under a condition covered by Rule 25-1 or in a water hazard.

Definitions

A ball is "lost" if:

a. It is not found or identified as his by the player within five minutes after the player's side or his or their caddies have begun to search for it; or

b. The player has put another ball into play under the Rules, even though he may not have searched for the original ball; or

c. The player has played any stroke with a <u>provisional ball</u> from the place where the original ball is likely to be or from a point nearer the hole than that place, whereupon the provisional ball becomes the <u>ball in play</u>.

Time spent in playing a <u>wrong ball</u> is not counted in the five-minute period allowed for search.

"Out of bounds" is ground on which play is prohibited.

When out of bounds is defined by reference to stakes or a fence, or as being beyond stakes or a fence, the out of bounds line is determined by the nearest inside points of the stakes or fence posts at ground level excluding angled supports.

When out of bounds is defined by a line on the ground, the line itself is out of bounds.

The out of bounds line extends vertically upwards and downwards.

A ball is out of bounds when all of it lies out of bounds.

A player may stand out of bounds to play a ball lying within bounds.

A "provisional ball" is a ball played under Rule 27-2 for a ball which may be <u>lost</u> outside a <u>water hazard</u> or may be <u>out of bounds</u>.

27-1   **Ball Lost or Out of Bounds**

If a ball is <u>lost</u> outside a <u>water hazard</u> or is <u>out of bounds</u>, the player shall play a ball, *under penalty of one stroke*, as nearly as possible at the spot from which the original ball was last played (see Rule 20-5).

> **PENALTY FOR BREACH OF RULE 27-1**
> *Match play — Loss of hole;*
> *Stroke play — Two strokes.*

27-2   **Provisional Ball**

a. PROCEDURE

If a ball may be <u>lost</u> outside a <u>water hazard</u> or may be <u>out of bounds</u>, to save time the player may play another ball provisionally as nearly as possible at the spot from which the original ball was played (see Rule 20-5). The player shall inform his opponent in match play or his marker or a fellow-competitor in stroke play that he intends to play a <u>provisional ball</u>, and he shall play it before he or his partner goes forward to search for the original ball. If he fails to do so and plays another ball, such ball is not a provisional ball and becomes the <u>ball in play</u> *under penalty of stroke and distance* (Rule 27-1); the original ball is deemed to be lost.

b. WHEN PROVISIONAL BALL BECOMES
BALL IN PLAY

The player may play a provisional ball until he reaches the place where the original ball is likely to be. If he plays a stroke with the provisional ball from the place where the original ball is likely to be or from a point nearer the hole than that place, the original ball is deemed to be <u>lost</u> and the provisional ball becomes the ball in play *under penalty of stroke and distance* (Rule 27-1).

If the original ball is lost outside a water hazard or is out of bounds, the provisional ball becomes the ball in play, *under penalty of stroke and distance* (Rule 27-1).

c. WHEN PROVISIONAL BALL TO BE ABANDONED

If the original ball is neither lost outside a water hazard nor out of bounds, the player shall abandon the provisional ball and continue play with the original ball. If he fails to do so, any further strokes played with the provisional ball shall constitute playing a <u>wrong ball</u> and the provisions of Rule 15 shall apply.

Note: If the original ball is in a water hazard, the player shall play the ball as it lies or proceed under Rule 26. If it is lost in a water hazard or unplayable, the player shall proceed under Rule 26 or 28, whichever is applicable.

Ball Unplayable

The player may declare his ball unplayable at any place on the course except when the ball is in a <u>water hazard</u>. The player is the sole judge as to whether his ball is unplayable.

If the player deems his ball to be unplayable, he shall, *under penalty of one stroke*:

a. Play a ball as nearly as possible at the spot from which the original ball was last played (see Rule 20-5);

   or

b. Drop a ball within two club-lengths of the spot where the ball lay, but not nearer the hole;

   or

c. Drop a ball behind the point where the ball lay, keeping that point directly between the hole and the spot on which the ball is dropped, with no limit to how far behind that point the ball may be dropped.

If the unplayable ball is in a <u>bunker</u>, the player may proceed under Clause a, b or c. If he elects to proceed under Clause b or c, a ball must be dropped in the bunker.

The ball may be cleaned when lifted under this Rule.

PENALTY FOR BREACH OF RULE:
Match play — Loss of hole;
Stroke play — Two strokes.

Other Forms of Play

Rule 29   **Threesomes and Foursomes**

Definitions

Threesome: A match in which one plays against two, and each side plays one ball.

Foursome: A match in which two play against two, and each side plays one ball.

29-1   **General**

In a threesome or a foursome, during any <u>stipulated round</u> the partners shall play alternately from the teeing grounds and alternately during the play of each hole. <u>Penalty strokes</u> do not affect the order of play.

29-2   **Match Play**

If a player plays when his partner should have played, *his side shall lose the hole.*

29-3   **Stroke Play**

If the partners play a stroke or strokes in incorrect order, such stroke or strokes shall be cancelled and *the side shall incur a penalty of two strokes.* The side shall correct the error by playing a ball in correct order as nearly as possible at the spot from which it first played in incorrect order (see Rule 20-5). If the side plays a stroke from the next <u>teeing ground</u> without first correcting the error or, in the case of the last hole of the round, leaves the <u>putting green</u> without declaring its intention to correct the error, *the side shall be disqualified.*

Three-Ball, Best-Ball and Four-Ball Match Play

Definitions

Three-Ball: A match play competition in which three play against one another, each playing his own ball. Each player is playing two distinct matches.

Best-Ball: A match in which one plays against the better ball of two or the best ball of three players.

Four-Ball: A match in which two play their better ball against the better ball of two other players.

30-1 Rules of Golf Apply

The Rules of Golf, so far as they are not at variance with the following special Rules, shall apply to three-ball, best-ball and four-ball matches.

30-2 Three-Ball Match Play

a. BALL AT REST MOVED BY AN OPPONENT

Except as otherwise provided in the Rules, if the player's ball is touched or moved by an opponent, his <u>caddie</u> or <u>equipment</u> other than during search, Rule 18-3b applies. *That opponent shall incur a penalty stroke in his match with the player,* but not in his match with the other opponent.

b. BALL DEFLECTED OR STOPPED
BY AN OPPONENT ACCIDENTALLY

If a player's ball is accidentally deflected or stopped by an opponent, his <u>caddie</u> or <u>equipment</u>, no penalty shall be incurred. In his match with that opponent the player may play the ball as it lies or, before another stroke is played by either side, he may cancel the stroke and play a ball without penalty as nearly as possible at the spot from which the original ball was last played (see Rule 20-5). In his match with the other opponent, the ball shall be played as it lies.

Exception: Ball striking person attending flagstick — see Rule 17-3b.

(Ball purposely deflected or stopped by opponent — see Rule 1-2.)

30-3 **Best-Ball and Four-Ball Match Play**

a. REPRESENTATION OF SIDE

A side may be represented by one partner for all or any part of a match; all partners need not be present. An absent partner may join a match between holes, but not during play of a hole.

b. MAXIMUM OF FOURTEEN CLUBS

The side shall be penalized for a breach of Rule 4-4 by any partner.

c. ORDER OF PLAY

Balls belonging to the same side may be played in the order the side considers best.

d. WRONG BALL

If a player plays a stroke with a <u>wrong ball</u> except in a <u>hazard</u>, *he shall be disqualified for that hole*, but his partner incurs no penalty even if the wrong ball belongs to him. If the wrong ball belongs to another player, its owner shall place a ball on the spot from which the wrong ball was first played.

e. DISQUALIFICATION OF SIDE

(i) *A side shall be disqualified* for a breach of any of the following by any partner:

Rule 1-3 — Agreement to Waive Rules.

Rule 4-1, -2 or -3 — Clubs.

Rule 5-1 or -2 — The Ball.

Rule 6-2a — Handicap
(playing off higher handicap).

Rule 6-4 — Caddie.

Rule 6-7 — Undue Delay;
Slow Play (repeated offense).

Rule 14-3 — Artificial Devices
and Unusual Equipment.

(ii) *A side shall be disqualified* for a breach of any of the following by all partners:

Rule 6-3 — Time of Starting
and Groups.

Rule 6-8 — Discontinuance of Play.

f. EFFECT OF OTHER PENALTIES

If a player's breach of a Rule assists his partner's play or adversely affects an opponent's play, *the partner incurs the applicable penalty in addition to any penalty incurred by the player.*

In all other cases where a player incurs a penalty for breach of a Rule, the penalty shall not apply to his partner. Where the penalty is stated to be loss of hole, the effect shall be to disqualify the player for that hole.

g. ANOTHER FORM OF MATCH
PLAYED CONCURRENTLY

In a best-ball or four-ball match when another form of match is played concurrently, the above special Rules shall apply.

Rule 31 **Four-Ball Stroke Play**

In four-ball stroke play two competitors play as partners, each playing his own ball. The lower score of the partners is the score for the hole. If one partner fails to complete the play of a hole, there is no penalty.

31-1 **Rules of Golf Apply**

The Rules of Golf, so far as they are not at variance with the following special Rules, shall apply to four-ball stroke play.

31-2 **Representation of Side**

A side may be represented by either partner for all or any part of a <u>stipulated round</u>; both partners need not be present. An absent competitor may join his partner between holes, but not during play of a hole.

31-3 **Maximum of Fourteen Clubs**

The side shall be penalized for a breach of Rule 4-4 by either partner.

31-4 **Scoring**

The marker is required to record for each hole only the gross score of whichever partner's score is to count. The gross scores to count must be individually identifiable; otherwise *the side shall be disqualified*. Only one of the partners need be responsible for complying with Rule 6-6b.

(Wrong score — see Rule 31-7a.)

31-5 **Order of Play**

Balls belonging to the same side may be played in the order the side considers best.

31-6 **Wrong Ball**

If a competitor plays a stroke or strokes with a <u>wrong ball</u> except in a <u>hazard</u>, *he shall add two penalty strokes to his score for the hole* and shall then play the correct ball. His partner incurs no penalty even if the wrong ball belongs to him.

If the wrong ball belongs to another competitor, its owner shall place a ball on the spot from which the wrong ball was first played.

31-7 **Disqualification Penalties**

a. BREACH BY ONE PARTNER

A side shall be disqualified from the competition for a breach of any of the following by either partner:

Rule 1-3 — Agreement to Waive Rules.

Rule 3-4 — Refusal to Comply with Rule.

Rule 4-1, -2 or -3 — Clubs.

Rule 5-1 or -2 — The Ball.

Rule 6-2b — Handicap (playing off higher handicap; failure to record handicap).

Rule 6-4 — Caddie.

Rule 6-6b — Signing and Returning Card.

Rule 6-6d — Wrong Score for Hole, i.e., when the recorded score of the partner whose score is to count is lower than actually taken. If the recorded score of the partner whose score is to count is higher than actually taken, it must stand as returned.

Rule 6-7 — Undue Delay; Slow Play (repeated offense).

Rule 7-1 — Practice Before or Between Rounds.

Rule 14-3 — Artificial Devices and Unusual Equipment.

> *Rule 31-4* — Gross Scores to Count Not
> Individually Identifiable.

b. BREACH BY BOTH PARTNERS
A side shall be disqualified:
(i)   for a breach by both partners of Rule 6-3
(Time of Starting and Groups) or Rule 6-
8 (Discontinuance of Play), or
(ii) if, at the same hole, each partner is in
breach of a Rule the penalty for which is
disqualification from the competition or
for a hole.

c. FOR THE HOLE ONLY
In all other cases where a breach of a Rule
would entail disqualification, *the competitor shall
be disqualified only for the hole at which the
breach occurred.*

31-8   Effect of Other Penalties
If a competitor's breach of a Rule assists his partner's play, *the partner incurs the applicable penalty in
addition to any penalty incurred by the competitor.*
In all other cases where a competitor incurs a
penalty for breach of a Rule, the penalty shall not
apply to his partner.

Rule 32   Bogey, Par and Stableford Competitions

32-1   Conditions
Bogey, par and Stableford competitions are
forms of stroke competition in which play is
against a fixed score at each hole. The Rules for
stroke play, so far as they are not at variance with
the following special Rules, apply.

a. Bogey and Par Competitions

The reckoning for bogey and par competitions is made as in match play. Any hole for which a competitor makes no return shall be regarded as a loss. The winner is the competitor who is most successful in the aggregate of holes.

The marker is responsible for marking only the gross number of strokes for each hole where the competitor makes a net score equal to or less than the fixed score.

Note: Maximum of 14 clubs — Penalties as in match play — see Rule 4-4.

b. Stableford Competitions

The reckoning in Stableford competitions is made by points awarded in relation to a fixed score at each hole as follows:

Hole Played In	Points
More than one over fixed score or no score returned	0
One over fixed score	1
Fixed score	2
One under fixed score	3
Two under fixed score	4
Three under fixed score	5
Four under fixed score	6

The winner is the competitor who scores the highest number of points.

The marker shall be responsible for marking only the gross number of strokes at each hole where the competitor's net score earns one or more points.

Note: Maximum of 14 clubs (Rule 4-4) — Penalties applied as follows: From total points scored for the round, deduction of two points for each hole at which any breach occurred; maximum deduction per round: four points.

32-2 **Disqualification Penalties**

a. FROM THE COMPETITION

A competitor shall be disqualified from the competition for a breach of any of the following:

Rule 1-3 — Agreement to Waive Rules.

Rule 3-4 — Refusal to Comply with Rule.

Rule 4-1, -2 or -3 — Clubs.

Rule 5-1 or -2 — The Ball.

Rule 6-2b — Handicap (playing off higher handicap; failure to record handicap).

Rule 6-3 — Time of Starting and Groups.

Rule 6-4 — Caddie.

Rule 6-6b — Signing and Returning Card.

Rule 6-6d — Wrong Score for Hole, except that no penalty shall be incurred when a breach of this Rule does not affect the result of the hole.

Rule 6-7 — Undue Delay; Slow Play (repeated offense).

Rule 6-8 — Discontinuance of Play.

Rule 7-1 — Practice Before or Between Rounds.

Rule 14-3 — Artificial Devices and Unusual Equipment.

b. FOR A HOLE

In all other cases where a breach of a Rule would entail disqualification, the competitor shall be disqualified only for the hole at which the breach occurred.

Administration

Rule 33   **The Committee**

33-1   **Conditions; Waiving Rule**

The Committee shall lay down the conditions under which a competition is to be played.

The Committee has no power to waive a Rule of Golf.

Certain special rules governing stroke play are so substantially different from those governing match play that combining the two forms of play is not practicable and is not permitted. The results of matches played and the scores returned in these circumstances shall not be accepted.

In stroke play the Committee may limit a referee's duties.

33-2   **The Course**

a. DEFINING BOUNDS AND MARGINS

The Committee shall define accurately:

(i)   the <u>course</u> and <u>out of bounds</u>,
(ii) the margins of <u>water hazards</u> and <u>lateral water hazards</u>,
(iii) <u>ground under repair</u>, and
(iv) <u>obstructions</u> and integral parts of the course.

b. NEW HOLES

New holes should be made on the day on which a stroke competition begins and at such other times as the Committee considers necessary, provided all competitors in a single round play with each hole cut in the same position.

Exception: When it is impossible for a damaged hole to be repaired so that it conforms with the Definition, the Committee may make a new hole in a nearby similar position.

Note: Where a single round is to be played on more than one day, the Committee may provide in the conditions of a competition that the holes and teeing grounds may be differently situated on each day of the competition, provided that, on any one day, all competitors play with each hole and each teeing ground in the same position.

c. PRACTICE GROUND

Where there is no practice ground available outside the area of a competition <u>course</u>, the Committee should lay down the area on which players may practice on any day of a competition, if it is practicable to do so. On any day of a stroke competition, the Committee should not normally permit practice on or to a <u>putting green</u> or from a <u>hazard</u> of the competition course.

d. COURSE UNPLAYABLE

If the Committee or its authorized representative considers that for any reason the course is not in a playable condition or that there are circumstances which render the proper playing of the game impossible, it may, in match play or stroke play, order a temporary suspension of play or, in stroke play, declare play null and void and cancel all scores for the round in question. When play has been temporarily suspended, it shall be resumed from where it was discontinued, even though resumption occurs on a subsequent day. When a round is cancelled, all penalties incurred in that round are cancelled.

(Procedure in discontinuing play — see Rule 6-8.)

33-3 **Times of Starting and Groups**

The Committee shall lay down the times of starting and, in stroke play, arrange the groups in which competitors shall play.

When a match play competition is played over an extended period, the Committee shall lay down the limit of time within which each round shall be completed. When players are allowed to arrange the date of their match within these limits, the Committee should announce that the match must be played at a stated time on the last day of the period unless the players agree to a prior date.

33-4 **Handicap Stroke Table**

The Committee shall publish a table indicating the order of holes at which handicap strokes are to be given or received.

33-5 **Score Card**

In stroke play, the Committee shall issue for each competitor a score card containing the date and the competitor's name or, in foursome or four-ball stroke play, the competitors' names.

In stroke play, the Committee is responsible for the addition of scores and application of the handicap recorded on the card.

In four-ball stroke play, the Committee is responsible for recording the better-ball score for each hole and in the process applying the handicaps recorded on the card, and adding the better-ball scores.

In bogey, par and Stableford competitions, the Committee is responsible for applying the handicap recorded on the card and determining the result of each hole and the overall result or points total.

33-6 **Decision of Ties**

The Committee shall announce the manner, day and time for the decision of a halved match or of a tie, whether played on level terms or under handicap.

A halved match shall not be decided by stroke play. A tie in stroke play shall not be decided by a match.

33-7 **Disqualification Penalty; Committee Discretion**

A penalty of disqualification may in exceptional individual cases be waived, modified or imposed if the Committee considers such action warranted.

Any penalty less than disqualification shall not be waived or modified.

33-8 **Local Rules**

a. POLICY

The Committee may make and publish Local Rules for abnormal conditions if they are consistent with the policy of the Governing Authority for the country concerned as set forth in Appendix I to these Rules.

b. WAIVING PENALTY

A penalty imposed by a Rule of Golf shall not be waived by a Local Rule.

Rule 34 Disputes and Decisions

34-1 Claims and Penalties

a. MATCH PLAY

In match play if a claim is lodged with the Committee under Rule 2-5, a decision should be given as soon as possible so that the state of the match may, if necessary, be adjusted.

If a claim is not made within the time limit provided by Rule 2-5, it shall not be considered unless it is based on facts previously unknown to the player making the claim and the player making the claim had been given wrong information (Rules 6-2a and 9) by an opponent. In any case, no later claim shall be considered after the result of the match has been officially announced, unless the Committee is satisfied that the opponent knew he was giving wrong information.

There is no time limit on applying the disqualification penalty for a breach of Rule 1-3.

b. STROKE PLAY

Except as provided below, in stroke play, no penalty shall be rescinded, modified or imposed after the competition has closed. A competition is deemed to have closed when the result has been officially announced or, in stroke play qualifying followed by match play, when the player has teed off in his first match.

Exceptions: A penalty of disqualification shall be imposed after the competition has closed if a competitor:

  (i) was in breach of Rule 1-3 (Agreement to Waive Rules); or

  (ii) returned a score card on which he had recorded a handicap which, before the competition closed, he knew was higher than that to which he was entitled, and this affected the number of strokes received (Rule 6-2b); or

(iii) returned a score for any hole lower than actually taken (Rule 6-6d) for any reason other than failure to include a penalty which, before the competition closed, he did not know he had incurred; or

(iv) knew, before the competition closed, that he had been in breach of any other Rule for which the prescribed penalty is disqualification.

34-2 **Referee's Decision**

If a referee has been appointed by the Committee, his decision shall be final.

34-3 **Committee's Decision**

In the absence of a referee, any dispute or doubtful point on the Rules shall be referred to the Committee, whose decision shall be final.

If the Committee cannot come to a decision, it shall refer the dispute or doubtful point to the Rules of Golf Committee of the United States Golf Association, whose decision shall be final.

If the dispute or doubtful point has not been referred to the Rules of Golf Committee, the player or players have the right to refer an agreed statement through the Secretary of the Club to the Rules of Golf Committee for an opinion as to the correctness of the decision given. The reply will be sent to the Secretary of the Club or Clubs concerned.

If play is conducted other than in accordance with the Rules of Golf, the Rules of Golf Committee will not give a decision on any question.

Appendix I

LOCAL RULES;
CONDITIONS OF
THE COMPETITION

Local Rules

Rule 33-8 provides:

"The Committee may make and publish Local Rules for abnormal conditions if they are consistent with the policy of the Governing Authority for the country concerned as set forth in Appendix I to these Rules.

"A penalty imposed by a Rule of Golf shall not be waived by a Local Rule."

Information regarding acceptable and prohibited Local Rules is provided in the *Decisions on the Rules of Golf* under Rule 33-8. Among the matters for which Local Rules may be advisable are the following:

1. Obstructions

Clarifying the status of objects which may be obstructions (Rule 24).

Declaring any construction to be an integral part of the course and, accordingly, not an obstruction, e.g., built-up sides of teeing grounds, putting greens and bunkers (Rules 24 and 33-2a).

2. Roads and Paths

Providing relief of the type afforded under Rule 24-2b from roads and paths not having artificial surfaces and sides if they could unfairly affect play.

3. Preservation of Course

Preservation of the course by defining areas, including turf nurseries and other parts of the course under cultivation, as ground under repair from which play is prohibited.

4. Water Hazards

Lateral Water Hazards. Clarifying the status of sections of water hazards which may be lateral water hazards (Rule 26).

Provisional Ball. Permitting play of a provisional ball for a ball which may be in a water hazard of such character that it would be impracticable to determine whether the ball is in the hazard or to do so would unduly delay play. In such case, if a provisional ball is played and the original ball is in a water hazard, the player may play the original ball as it lies or continue the provisional ball in play, but he may not proceed under Rule 26-1.

5. Defining Bounds and Margins

Specifying means used to define out of bounds, hazards, water hazards, lateral water hazards and ground under repair.

6. Ball Drops

Establishment of special areas on which balls may be dropped when it is not feasible or practicable to proceed exactly in conformity with Rule 24-2b (immovable obstructions), Rule 25-1b or -1c (ground under repair), Rule 26-1 (water hazards and lateral water hazards) and Rule 28 (ball unplayable).

7. Temporary Conditions — Mud, Extreme Wetness

Temporary conditions which might interfere with proper playing of the game, including mud and extreme wetness warranting lifting an embedded ball anywhere through the green (see detailed recommendation below) or removal of mud from a ball through the green.

* * *

Following are the suggested texts for other Local Rules which are authorized by the USGA:

Lifting an Embedded Ball

Rule 25-2 provides relief without penalty for a ball embedded in its own pitch-mark in any closely mown area through the green.

On the putting green, a ball may be lifted and damage caused by the impact of a ball may be repaired (Rules 16-1b and c).

When permission to lift an embedded ball anywhere through the green would be warranted, the following Local Rule is suggested:

> Anywhere "through the green," a ball which is embedded in its own pitch-mark in the ground, except in loose sand, may be lifted without penalty, cleaned and dropped as near as possible to the spot where it lay but not nearer the hole. (See Rule 20.) The ball when dropped must first strike a part of the course through the green.
>
> ("Through the green" is the whole area of the course except:
>
> a.   Teeing ground and putting green of the hole being played;
>
> b.   All hazards on the course.)

Exception: A player may not obtain relief under this Rule if it is clearly unreasonable for him to play a stroke because of interference by anything other than the condition covered by this Rule.

Practice Between Holes

When, between the play of two holes, it is desired to prohibit practice putting or chipping on or near the putting green of the hole last played, the following Local Rule is recommended:

> Between the play of two holes, a player shall not play any practice stroke on or near the putting green of the hole last played. (For other practice, see Rules 7 and 33-2c.)

> **PENALTY FOR BREACH OF LOCAL RULE:**
> *Match play — Loss of next hole;*
> *Stroke play — Two strokes at next hole.*

Marking Position of Lifted Ball

When it is desired to require a specific means of marking the position of a lifted ball on the putting green, the following Local Rule is recommended:

> Before a ball on the putting green is lifted, its position shall be marked by placing a small coin or some similar object immediately behind the ball; if the ball-marker interferes with another player, it should be moved one or more putterhead-lengths to one side. If the position of the ball is not so marked, *the player shall incur a penalty of one stroke* and the ball shall be replaced. If the ball is not replaced, *the player shall incur the penalty* for breach of Rule 20-3a, but no additional penalty under this Local Rule shall be applied. (This modifies Rule 20-1.)

Prohibition Against Touching Line of Putt with Club

When it is desired to prohibit touching the line of putt with a club in moving loose impediments, the following Local Rule is recommended:

The line of putt shall not be touched with a club
for any purpose except to repair old hole plugs or ball
marks or during address. (This modifies Rule 16-1a.)

PENALTY FOR BREACH OF LOCAL RULE:
Match play — Loss of hole;
Stroke play — Two strokes.

Protection of Young Trees

When it is desired to prevent damage to young trees,
the following Local Rule is recommended:

Protection of young trees identified by _____
— If such a tree interferes with a player's stance or
the area of his intended swing, the ball must be
lifted, without penalty, and dropped in accordance
with the procedure prescribed in Rule 24-2b
(Immovable Obstruction). If the ball is in a water
hazard, the player shall lift and drop the ball in
accordance with Rule 24-2b(i) except that the ball
must be dropped in the water hazard or the player
may proceed under Rule 26-1, if applicable. The
ball may be cleaned when so lifted.

Exception: A player may not obtain relief under
this Rule if (a) it is clearly unreasonable for him to
play a stroke because of interference by anything
other than such tree, or (b) interference by such
tree would occur only through use of an unnecessarily abnormal stance, swing or direction of play.

Environmentally-Sensitive Areas

When the Committee is required to prohibit play from
environmentally-sensitive areas which are on or adjoin the
course, the following Local Rule is recommended:

1. Definition

An environmentally-sensitive area is an area so declared by an appropriate authority, entry into and/or play from which is prohibited for environmental reasons. Such an area may be defined as ground under repair, a water hazard, a lateral water hazard or out of bounds at the discretion of the Committee provided that, in the case of an environmentally-sensitive area which has been defined as a water hazard or a lateral water hazard, the area is, by Definition, a water hazard.

Note: The Committee may not declare an area to be environmentally-sensitive.

2. Ball in Environmentally-Sensitive Area

a. GROUND UNDER REPAIR

If a ball is in an environmentally-sensitive area which is defined as ground under repair, a ball must be dropped in accordance with Rule 25-1b.

If there is reasonable evidence that a ball is lost within an environmentally-sensitive area which is defined as ground under repair, the player may take relief without penalty as prescribed in Rule 25-1c.

b. WATER HAZARDS AND LATERAL WATER HAZARDS

If a ball is in or there is reasonable evidence that it is lost in an environmentally-sensitive area which is defined as a water hazard or a lateral water hazard, the player must, under penalty of one stroke, proceed under Rule 26-1.

c. OUT OF BOUNDS

If a ball is in an environmentally-sensitive area which is defined as out of bounds, the player shall play a ball, under penalty of one stroke, as nearly as possible at the spot from which the original ball was last played (see Rule 20-5).

3. Interference with Stance or Area of Intended Swing

Interference by an environmentally-sensitive area occurs when such a condition interferes with the player's stance or the area of his intended swing. If interference exists, the player must take relief as follows:

(i) *Through the Green:* If the ball lies through the green, the point on the course nearest to where the ball lies shall be determined which (a) is not nearer the hole, (b) avoids interference by the condition and (c) is not in a hazard or on a putting green. The player shall lift the ball and drop it without penalty within one club-length of the point thus determined on a part of the course which fulfills (a), (b) and (c) above.

(ii) *In a Hazard:* If the ball is in a hazard, the player shall lift the ball and drop it either:

(a) Without penalty, in the hazard, as near as possible to the spot where the ball lay, but not nearer the hole, on a part of the course which provides complete relief from the condition; or

(b) Under penalty of one stroke, outside the hazard, keeping the point where the ball lay directly between the hole and the spot on which the ball is dropped, with no limit to how far behind the hazard the ball may be dropped. Additionally, the player may proceed under Rule 26 or 28 if applicable.

(iii) *On the putting green:* If the ball lies on the putting green, the player shall lift the ball and place it without penalty in the nearest position to where it lay which affords complete relief from the condition, but not nearer the hole or in a hazard.

The ball may be cleaned when so lifted under Clause 3 of this Local Rule.

Exception: A player may not obtain relief under Clause 3 of this Local Rule if (a) it is clearly unreasonable for him to play a stroke because of interference by anything other than a condition covered by this Local Rule or (b) interference by such a condition would occur only through use of an unnecessarily abnormal stance, swing or direction of play.

4. Re-Dropping

If a dropped ball rolls into a position covered by this Local Rule or a position covered by 20-2c, it shall be re-dropped without penalty. If the ball when re-dropped rolls into such a position, it shall be placed as near as possible to the spot where it first struck a part of the course when re-dropped.

PENALTY FOR BREACH OF RULE:
Match play — Loss of hole;
Stroke play — Two strokes.

Note: In the case of a serious breach of this Local Rule, the Committee may impose a penalty of disqualification.

Temporary Obstructions

When temporary obstructions are installed for a competition, the following Local Rule is recommended:

1. Definition

Temporary immovable obstructions include tents, scoreboards, grandstands, refreshment stands and lavatories. Any temporary equipment for photography, press, radio and television is also a temporary immovable obstruction, provided it is not mobile or otherwise readily movable.

Excluded are temporary power lines and cables and mats covering them and temporary telephone lines and stanchions supporting them (from which relief is provided in Clause 5) and mobile or otherwise readily movable equipment for photography, press, radio or television (from which relief is obtainable under Rule 24-1).

2. Interference

Interference by a temporary immovable obstruction occurs when (a) the ball lies in or on the obstruction or so close to the obstruction that the obstruction interferes with the player's stance or the area of his intended swing or (b) the obstruction intervenes between the player's ball and the hole or the ball lies within one club-length of a spot where such intervention would exist.

3. Relief

A player may obtain relief from interference by a temporary immovable obstruction as follows:

a. THROUGH THE GREEN

Through the green, the point on the course nearest to where the ball lies shall be determined which (a) is not nearer the hole, (b) avoids interference as defined in Clause 2 of this Local Rule and (c) is not in a hazard or on a putting green. He shall lift the ball and drop it without penalty within one club-length of the point thus determined on ground which fulfills (a), (b) and (c) above. The ball may be cleaned when so lifted.

b. IN A HAZARD

If the ball lies in a hazard, the player shall lift and drop the ball either:

(i) in the hazard, without penalty, on the nearest ground affording complete relief within the limits specified in Clause 3a above or, if complete relief is impossible, on ground within the hazard affording maximum relief, or

(ii) outside the hazard, *under penalty of one stroke*, as follows: The player shall determine the point on the course nearest to where the ball lies which (a) is not nearer the hole, (b) avoids interference as defined in Clause 2 of this Local Rule and (c) is not in a hazard. He shall drop the ball within one club-length of the point thus determined on ground which fulfills (a), (b) and (c) above.

The ball may be cleaned when so lifted.

Exception: A player may not obtain relief from a temporary immovable obstruction under Clause 3a or 3b if (a) it is clearly unreasonable for him to play a stroke, or in the case of intervention to play a stroke directly toward the hole, because of interference by anything other than the obstruction, (b) interference would occur only through use of an unnecessarily abnormal stance, swing or direction of play, or (c) in the case of intervention, it would be clearly unreasonable to expect the player to be able to strike the ball far enough toward the hole to reach the obstruction.

4. Ball Lost in Temporary Immovable Obstruction

If there is reasonable evidence that a ball is lost within the confines of a temporary immovable obstruction, the player may take relief without penalty as prescribed in Rule 24-2c.

5. Temporary Power Lines and Cables

The above Clauses do not apply to (1) temporary power lines or cables or mats covering them or (2) temporary telephone lines or stanchions supporting them. If such items are readily movable, the player may obtain relief under Rule 24-1. If they are not readily movable, the player may, if the ball lies through the green, obtain relief as provided in Rule 24-2b(i). If the ball lies in a bunker or a water hazard, the player may obtain relief under Rule 24-2b(i), except that the ball must be dropped in the bunker or water hazard.

Note: The prohibition in Rule 24-2b(i) against crossing over, through or under the obstruction does not apply.

If a ball strikes a temporary power line or cable which is elevated, it must be replayed, without penalty (see Rule 20-5). If the ball is not immediately recoverable, another ball may be substituted.

Exception: Ball striking elevated junction section of cable rising from the ground shall not be replayed.

6. Re-Dropping

If a dropped ball rolls into a position covered by this Local Rule or a position covered by Rule 20-2c, it shall be re-dropped without penalty. If the ball when re-dropped rolls into such a position, it shall be placed as near as possible to the spot where it first struck a part of the course when re-dropped.

PENALTY FOR BREACH OF LOCAL RULE:
Match play — Loss of hole;
Stroke play — Two strokes.

"Preferred Lies" and "Winter Rules"

The USGA does not endorse "preferred lies" and "winter rules" and recommends that the Rules of Golf be observed uniformly. Ground under repair is provided for in Rule 25. Occasional abnormal conditions which might interfere with fair play and are not widespread should be defined accurately as ground under repair.

However, adverse conditions are sometimes so general throughout a course that the Committee believes "preferred lies" or "winter rules" would promote fair play or help protect the course. Heavy snows, spring thaws, prolonged rains

or extreme heat can make fairways unsatisfactory and sometimes prevent use of heavy mowing equipment.

When a Committee adopts a Local Rule for "preferred
lies" or "winter rules," it should be in detail and should be
interpreted by the Committee, as there is no established
code for "winter rules." Without a detailed Local Rule, it
is meaningless for a Committee to post a notice merely
saying "Winter Rules Today."

The following Local Rule would seem appropriate for
the conditions in question, but the USGA will not inter-
pret it:

> A ball lying on a "fairway" may be lifted and
> cleaned, without penalty, and placed within one
> club-length of where it originally lay, not nearer
> the hole, and so as to preserve as nearly as possible
> the stance required to play from the original lie. A
> ball so lifted is back in play when the player
> addresses it or, if he does not address it, when he
> makes his next stroke at it.

Before a Committee adopts a Local Rule permitting
"preferred lies" or "winter rules," the following facts
should be considered:

1. Such a Local Rule conflicts with the Rules of
   Golf and the fundamental principle of playing
   the ball as it lies.

2. "Winter rules" are sometimes adopted under the
   guise of protecting the course when, in fact, the
   practical effect is just the opposite — they permit
   moving the ball to the best turf, from which divots are then taken to injure the course further.

3. "Preferred lies" or "winter rules" tend generally to
   lower scores and handicaps, thus penalizing the

players in competition with players whose scores
for handicaps are made under the Rules of Golf.

4. Extended use or indiscriminate use of "preferred
lies" or "winter rules" will place players at a dis-
advantage when competing at a course where the
ball must be played as it lies.

Handicapping and "Preferred Lies"

Scores made under a Local Rule for "preferred
lies" or "winter rules" may be accepted for handicapping if the Committee considers that conditions warrant.

When such a Local Rule is adopted, the Committee should ensure that the course's normal scoring
difficulty is maintained as nearly as possible through
adjustment of tee-markers and related methods.
However, if extreme conditions cause extended use
of "preferred lies" or "winter rules" and the course
management cannot adjust scoring difficulty properly, the club should obtain a Temporary Course
Rating from its district golf association.

Conditions of the Competition

Rule 33-1 states: "The Committee shall lay down the conditions under which a competition is to be played." Conditions should include such matters as method of entry, eligibility requirements, format, the method of deciding ties, the method of determining the draw for match play and handicap allowances for a handicap competition.

How to Decide Ties

Rule 33-6 empowers the Committee to determine how and when a halved match or a stroke play tie shall be decided. The decision should be published in advance.

The USGA recommends:

1. **Match Play**

   A match which ends all square should be played off hole by hole until one side wins a hole. The play-off should start on the hole where the match began. In a handicap match, handicap strokes should be allowed as in the prescribed round.

2. **Stroke Play**

   (a) In the event of a tie in a scratch stroke play competition, an 18-hole play-off is recommended. If that is not feasible, a hole-by-hole play-off is recommended.

   (b) In the event of a tie in a handicap stroke play competition, a play-off over 18 holes with handicaps is recommended. If a shorter play-off is necessary, the percentage of 18 holes to be played should be applied to the players' handicaps to determine their play-off handicaps. It is advisable to arrange for a percentage of holes that will result in whole numbers in handicaps; if this is not feasible, handicap stroke fractions of one-half stroke or more should count as a full stroke and any lesser fraction should be disregarded.

(c) In either a scratch or handicap stroke play competition, if a play-off of any type is not feasible, matching score cards is recommended. The method of matching cards should be announced in advance. An acceptable method of matching cards is to determine the winner on the basis of the best score for the last nine holes. If the tying players have the same score for the last nine, determine the winner on the basis of the last six holes, last three holes and finally the 18th hole. If such a method is used in a handicap stroke play competition, one-half, one-third, one-sixth, etc., of the handicaps should be deducted.

(d) If the conditions of the competition provide that ties shall be decided over the last nine, last six, last three and last hole, they should also provide what will happen if this procedure does not produce a winner.

Draw for Match Play

Although the draw for match play may be completely blind or certain players may be distributed through different quarters or eighths, the General Numerical Draw is recommended if flights are determined by a qualifying round.

General Numerical Draw

For purposes of determining places in the draw, ties in qualifying rounds other than those for the last qualifying place shall be decided by the order in which scores are returned, the first score to be returned receiving the lowest available number, etc. If it is impossible to determine the order in which scores are returned, ties shall be determined by a blind draw.

UPPER HALF	LOWER HALF	UPPER HALF	LOWER HALF
64 QUALIFIERS		32 QUALIFIERS	
1 vs. 64	2 vs. 63	1 vs. 32	2 vs. 31
32 vs. 33	31 vs. 34	16 vs. 17	15 vs. 18
16 vs. 49	15 vs. 50	8 vs. 25	7 vs. 26
17 vs. 48	18 vs. 47	9 vs. 24	10 vs. 23
8 vs. 57	7 vs. 58	4 vs. 29	3 vs. 30
25 vs. 40	26 vs. 39	13 vs. 20	14 vs. 19
9 vs. 56	10 vs. 55	5 vs. 28	6 vs. 27
24 vs. 41	23 vs. 42	12 vs. 21	11 vs. 22
4 vs. 61	3 vs. 62	16 QUALIFIERS	
29 vs. 36	30 vs. 35	1 vs. 16	2 vs. 15
13 vs. 52	14 vs. 51	8 vs. 9	7 vs. 10
20 vs. 45	19 vs. 46	4 vs. 13	3 vs. 14
5 vs. 60	6 vs. 59	5 vs. 12	6 vs. 11
28 vs. 37	27 vs. 38	8 QUALIFIERS	
12 vs. 53	11 vs. 54	1 vs. 8	2 vs. 7
21 vs. 44	22 vs. 43	4 vs. 5	3 vs. 6

Handicap Allowances

The USGA recommends the following handicap allowances in handicap competitions:

Singles match play: Allow the higher-handi-capped player the full difference between the handicaps of the two players.

Four-ball match play: Reduce the handicaps of all four players by the handicap of the low-handicapped player, who shall then play from scratch. Allow each of the three other players 100 percent of the resulting difference.

Individual stroke play: Allow the full handicap.

Four-ball stroke play: Men — Allow each competitor 90 percent of his handicap. Women — Allow each competitor 95 percent of her handicap.

Best-ball-of-four, stroke play: Men — Allow each competitor 80 percent of his handicap. Women — Allow each competitor 90 percent of her handicap.

Optional Conditions

The following are some conditions which a Committee may wish to make:

List of Conforming Golf Balls

The USGA periodically issues a List of Conforming Golf Balls. If it is desired to require use of a brand of golf ball on the List, the List should be posted and the following issued as a condition of the competition:

Only brands of golf balls on the USGA's latest List of Conforming Golf Balls may be used. Penalty for use of brand not on the List: Disqualification.

One-Ball Rule

If it is desired to prohibit changing brands of golf balls during a stipulated round, the following condition is recommended; it is suggested that it be considered only for competitions involving expert players:

Limitation on Golf Balls Used During Round
(Condition: Rules 5-1 and 33-1)

1. BALLS WITH IDENTICAL MARKINGS TO BE USED

    During a stipulated round, the balls a player uses must be of the same brand and type as detailed by a single entry on the current list of Conforming Golf Balls.

PENALTY FOR BREACH OF CONDITION:

Match play — At the conclusion of the hole at which the breach is discovered, the state of the match shall be adjusted by deducting one hole for each hole at which a breach occurred. Maximum deduction per round: two holes. Stroke play — Two strokes for each hole at which any breach occurred; maximum penalty per round: four strokes.

2. PROCEDURE WHEN BREACH DISCOVERED

    When a player discovers that he has used a ball in breach of this condition, he shall abandon that ball before playing from the next teeing ground and complete the round using a proper ball; otherwise, *the player shall be disqualified.* If discovery is made during play of a hole and the player elects to substitute a proper ball before completing that hole, the player shall place a proper ball on the spot where the ball used in breach of this condition lay.

Time of Starting

If the Committee desires to adopt the condition in the Note under Rule 6-3a, the following wording is recommended:

Rule 6-3a provides: "The player shall start at the time laid down by the Committee." The penalty for breach of Rule 6-3a is disqualification. However, it is a condition of the competition that, if the player arrives at his starting point, ready to play, within five minutes after his starting time, in the absence of circumstances which warrant waiving the penalty of disqualification as provided in Rule 33-7, the penalty for failure to start on time is loss of the first hole in match play or two strokes at the first hole in stroke play instead of disqualification.

Discontinuance of Play

If the Committee desires to adopt the condition in the Note under Rule 6-8b, the following wording is recommended:

Rule 6-8b details the procedure for discontinuance of play. The penalty for a breach of Rule 6-8b is disqualification. However, it is a condition of the competition that, in potentially dangerous situations, play shall be discontinued immediately following a suspension of play by the Committee. If a player fails to discontinue play immediately, he shall be disqualified unless circumstances warrant waiving such penalty as provided in Rule 33-7. An immediate suspension of play will be signalled by a prolonged note of the siren.

Practice

The Committee may make regulations governing practice in accordance with the Note to Rule 7-1, Clause (c) of the Exception under Rule 7-2 and Rule 33-2c.

Advice in Team Competitions

If the Committee desires to adopt the condition in the Note under Rule 8, which applies to a team competition with or without concurrent individual competition, the following wording is recommended:

In accordance with the Note to Rule 8 of the Rules of Golf, each team may appoint one person (in addition to the persons from whom advice may be asked under Rule 8-1) who may give advice (including pointing out a line for putting) to members of that team. Such person [if it is desired to put a restriction on who may be appointed and/or permissible conduct of that person, insert such restriction here] shall be identified to the Committee before giving advice.

Automotive Transportation

If it is desired to prohibit automotive transportation in a competition, the following condition is suggested:

Players shall not use automotive transportation during play.

PENALTY FOR BREACH OF CONDITION:
Match play — At the conclusion of the hole at which the breach is discovered, the state of the match shall be adjusted by deducting one hole for each hole at which a breach occurred. Maximum deduction per round: two holes

Stroke play — Two strokes for each hole at which any breach occurred; maximum penalty per round: four strokes. In the event of a breach between the play of two holes, the penalty applies to the next hole.
Match or stroke play — Use of any unauthorized automotive vehicle shall be discontinued immediately upon discovery that a breach has occurred. Otherwise, the player shall be disqualified.

Appendices II and III

Any design in a club or ball which is not covered by Rules 4 and 5 and Appendices II and III, or which might significantly change the nature of the game, will be ruled on by the United States Golf Association and the Royal and Ancient Golf Club of St. Andrews.

Appendix II
DESIGN OF CLUBS

Design of Clubs

Clubs must not be substantially different from the traditional and customary form and make.

Rule 4-1 prescribes general regulations for their design. The following paragraphs, which provide some specifications and clarify how Rule 4-1 is interpreted, should be read in conjunction with that Rule.

Where a club, or part of a club, is required to have some specific property, this means that it must be designed and manufactured with the intention of having that property. The finished club or part must have that property within manufacturing tolerances appropriate to the material used.

4-1a   **General**

ADJUSTABILITY — EXCEPTION FOR PUTTERS

Clubs other than putters shall not be designed to be adjustable except for weight.

Some other forms of adjustability are permitted in the design of a putter, provided that:

   (i)   the adjustment cannot be readily made;
   (ii) all adjustable parts are firmly fixed and there is no reasonable likelihood of them working loose during a round; and
   (iii) all configurations of adjustment conform with the Rules.

The disqualification penalty for purposely changing the playing characteristics of a club during a <u>stipulated round</u> (Rule 4-2) applies to all clubs including a putter.

Note: It is recommended that all putters with adjustable parts be submitted to the United States Golf Association for a ruling.

4-1b **Shaft**

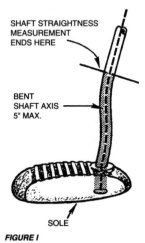

SHAFT STRAIGHTNESS MEASUREMENT ENDS HERE

BENT SHAFT AXIS 5" MAX.

SOLE

FIGURE I

STRAIGHTNESS

The shaft shall be straight from the top of the grip to a point not more than 5 inches (127 mm) above the sole, measured from the point where the shaft ceases to be straight along the axis of the bent part of the shaft and the neck and/or socket (see Fig. I).

LENGTH

The overall length of the club shall be at least 18 inches (457 mm) measured from the top of the grip along the axis of the shaft or a straight line extension of it to the sole of the club.

ALIGNMENT

When the club is in its normal address position the shaft shall be so aligned that:

(i) the projection of the straight part of the shaft onto the vertical plane through the toe and heel shall diverge from the vertical by at least 10 degrees (see Fig. II);

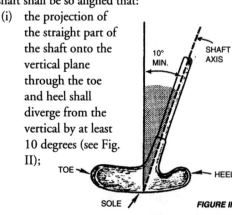

10° MIN.

SHAFT AXIS

TOE

HEEL

SOLE

FIGURE II

(ii) the projection of the straight part of the shaft onto the vertical plane along the intended line of play shall not diverge from the vertical by more than 20 degrees (see Fig. III).

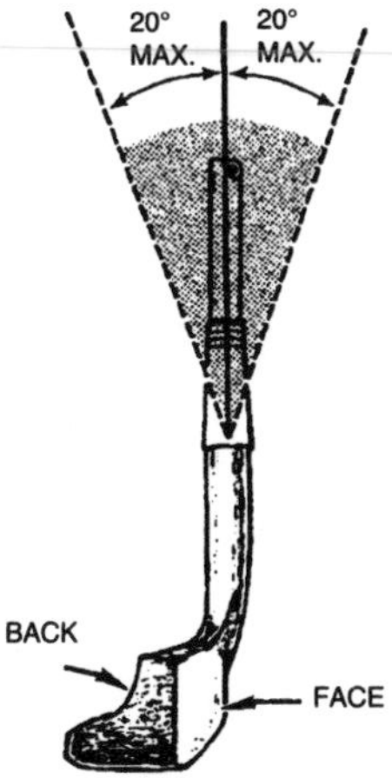

20° MAX.   20° MAX.

BACK

FACE

FIGURE III

Except for putters, all of the heel portion of the club shall lie within 0.625 inches (16 mm) of the plane containing the axis of the straight part of the shaft and the intended (horizontal) line of play (see Fig. IV).

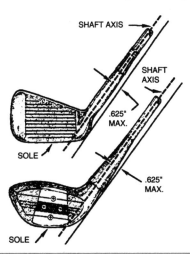

SHAFT AXIS

SHAFT AXIS

.625" MAX.

SOLE

.625" MAX.

FIGURE IV   SOLE

BENDING AND TWISTING PROPERTIES

At any point along its length, the shaft shall:

(i) bend in such a way that the deflection is the same regardless of how the shaft is rotated about its longitudinal axis; and

(ii) twist the same amount in both directions.

ATTACHMENT TO CLUBHEAD

The shaft shall be attached to the clubhead at the heel either directly or through a neck and/or socket. The length from the top of the neck and/or socket to the sole of the club shall not exceed 5 inches (127 mm), measured along the axis of, and following any bend in, the neck and/or socket (see Fig. V).

Exception for Putters: The shaft or neck or socket of a putter may be fixed at any point in the head.

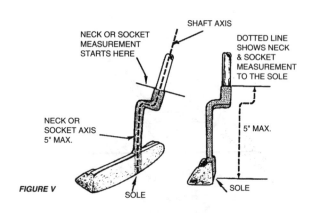

NECK OR SOCKET MEASUREMENT STARTS HERE

SHAFT AXIS

DOTTED LINE SHOWS NECK & SOCKET MEASUREMENT TO THE SOLE

NECK OR SOCKET AXIS 5" MAX.

5" MAX.

FIGURE V

SOLE

SOLE

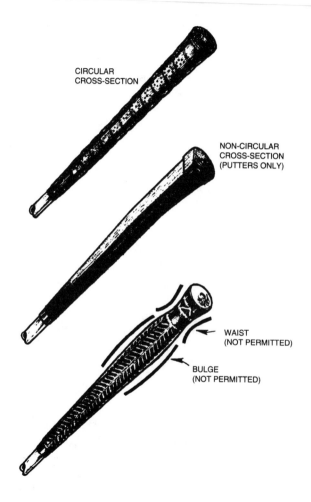

CIRCULAR
CROSS-SECTION

NON-CIRCULAR
CROSS-SECTION
(PUTTERS ONLY)

WAIST
(NOT PERMITTED)

BULGE
(NOT PERMITTED)

FIGURE VI

4-1c **Grip**

    (i) For clubs other than putters the grip must be circular in cross-section, except that a continuous, straight, slightly raised rib may be incorporated along the full length of the grip, and a slightly indented spiral is permitted on a wrapped grip or a replica of one.

    (ii) A putter grip may have a non-circular cross-section, provided the cross-section has no concavity, is symmetrical and remains generally similar throughout the length of the grip.

    (iii) The grip may be tapered but must not have any bulge or waist. Its cross-sectional dimension measured in any direction must not exceed 1.75 inches (45 mm).

    (iv) For clubs other than putters the axis of the grip must coincide with the axis of the shaft.

    (v) A putter may have more than one grip, provided each is circular in cross-section and the axis of each coincides with the axis of the shaft.

4-1d **Clubhead**

DIMENSIONS

The dimensions of a clubhead are measured, with the clubhead in its normal address position, on horizontal lines between vertical projections of the outermost points of (i) the heel and the toe and (ii) the face and the back (see Fig. VII, dimension A). If the outermost point of the heel is not clearly defined, it is deemed to be 0.625 inches (16 mm) above the horizontal plane on which the club is resting in its normal address position (see Fig. VII, dimension B).

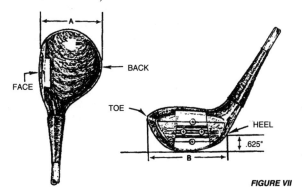

FIGURE VII

PLAIN IN SHAPE

The clubhead shall be generally plain in shape. All parts shall be rigid, structural in nature and functional. It is not practicable to define plain in shape precisely and comprehensively but features which are deemed to be in breach of this requirement and are therefore not permitted include:

a)   holes through the head,

b)   transparent material added for other than decorative or structural purposes,

c)   appendages to the main body of the head such as knobs, plates, rods or fins,

for the purpose of meeting dimensional specifications, for aiming or for any other purpose. Exceptions may be made for putters.

Any furrows in or runners on the sole shall not extend into the face.

4-1e **Club Face**

GENERAL

The material and construction of the face shall not have the effect at impact of a spring, or impart significantly more spin to the ball than a standard steel face, or have any other effect which would unduly influence the movement of the ball.

IMPACT AREA ROUGHNESS AND MATERIAL

Except for markings specified in the following paragraphs, the surface roughness within the area where impact is intended (the "impact area") must not exceed that of decorative sandblasting, or of fine milling.

The impact area must be of a single material. Exceptions may be made for wooden clubs (see Fig. VIII, illustrative impact area).

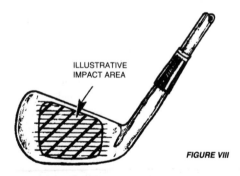

ILLUSTRATIVE
IMPACT AREA

FIGURE VIII

IMPACT AREA MARKINGS

Markings in the impact area must not have sharp edges or raised lips, as determined by a finger

test. Grooves or punch marks in the impact area
must meet the following specifications:

 (i) *Grooves.* A series of straight grooves with
diverging sides and a symmetrical cross-section may be used (see Fig. IX). The width
and cross-section must be consistent across
the face of the club and along the length of
the grooves. Any rounding of groove edges
shall be in the form of a radius which does
not exceed 0.020 inches (0.5 mm). The
width of the grooves shall not exceed 0.035
inches (0.9 mm), using the 30 degree
method of measurement on file with the
United States Golf Association. The distance between edges of adjacent grooves
must not be less than three times the width
of a groove, and not less than 0.075 inches
(1.9 mm). The depth of a groove must not
exceed 0.020 inches (0.5 mm).

Note: Exception - see US Decision 4-1/100.

 (ii) *Punch Marks.* Punch marks may be used.
The area of any such mark must not
exceed 0.0044 square inches (2.8 sq.

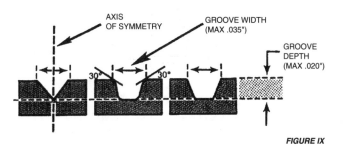

FIGURE IX

mm). A mark must not be closer to an adjacent mark than 0.168 inches (4.3 mm) measured from center to center. The depth of a punch mark must not exceed 0.040 inches (1.0 mm). If punch marks are used in combination with grooves, a punch mark must not be closer to a groove than 0.168 inches (4.3 mm), measured from center to center.

DECORATIVE MARKINGS

The center of the impact area may be indicated by a design within the boundary of a square whose sides are 0.375 inches (9.5 mm) in length. Such a design must not unduly influence the movement of the ball. Decorative markings are permitted outside the impact area.

NON-METALLIC CLUB FACE MARKINGS

The above specifications apply to clubs on which the impact area of the face is of metal or a material of similar hardness. They do not apply to clubs with faces made of other materials and whose loft angle is 24 degrees or less, but markings which could unduly influence the movement of the ball are prohibited. Clubs with this type of face and a loft angle exceeding 24 degrees may have grooves of maximum width 0.040 inches (1.00 mm) and maximum depth 1½ times the groove width, but must otherwise conform to the markings specifications above.

PUTTER FACE MARKINGS

The specifications above with regard to club face markings and surface roughness do not apply to putters.

APPENDIX III
THE BALL

The Ball

a. Weight

The weight of the ball shall not be greater than 1.620 ounces avoirdupois (45.93 gm).

b. Size

The diameter of the ball shall be not less than 1.680 inches (42.67 mm). This specification will be satisfied if, under its own weight, a ball falls through a 1.680 inches diameter ring gauge in fewer than 25 out of 100 randomly selected positions, the test being carried out at a temperature of $23\pm1°C$.

c. Spherical Symmetry

The ball must not be designed, manufactured or intentionally modified to have properties which differ from those of a spherically symmetrical ball.

d. Initial Velocity

The velocity of the ball shall not be greater than 250 feet (76.2 m) per second when measured on apparatus approved by the United States Golf Association. A maximum tolerance of 2% will be allowed. The temperature of the ball when tested shall be $23\pm1°C$.

e. Overall Distance Standard

A brand of golf ball, when tested on apparatus approved by the USGA on the outdoor range at the USGA Headquarters under the conditions set forth in the Overall Distance Standard for golf balls on file with the USGA, shall not cover an average distance in carry and roll exceeding 280 yards (256 m) plus a tolerance of 6%.

Note: The 6% tolerance will be reduced to a minimum of 4% as test techniques are improved.

Par Computation

"Par" is the score that an expert golfer would be expected to make for a given hole. Par means errorless play without flukes and under ordinary weather conditions, allowing two strokes on the putting green.

Yardages for guidance in computing par are given below. They should not be applied arbitrarily; allowance should be made for the configuration of the ground, any difficult or unusual conditions and the severity of the hazards.

Each hole should be measured horizontally from the middle of the tee area to be used to the center of the green, following the line of play planned by the architect in laying out the hole. Thus, in a hole with a bend, the line at the elbow point should be centered in the fairway in accordance with the architect's intention.

YARDAGES FOR GUIDANCE

Par	Men	Women
3	up to 250	up to 210
4	251 to 470	211 to 400
5	471 and over	401 to 575
6		576 and over

Flagstick Dimensions

The USGA recommends that the flagstick be at least seven feet in height and that its diameter be not greater than three-quarters of an inch from a point three inches above the ground to the bottom of the hole.

Protection of Persons Against Lightning

As there have been many deaths and injuries from lightning on golf courses, all clubs and sponsors of golf competitions are urged to take precaution for the protection of persons against lightning.

Attention is called to Rules 6-8 and 33-2d.

The USGA suggests that players be informed that they have the right to stop play if they think lightning threatens them, even though the Committee may not have specifically authorized it by signal.

The USGA generally uses the following signals and recommends that all Committees do similarly:

Discontinue Play Immediately: One prolonged note of siren.

Discontinue Play: Three consecutive notes of siren, repeated.

Resume Play: Two short notes of siren, repeated.

Posters containing detailed information on protection from lightning are available from the USGA.

RULES OF
AMATEUR STATUS

Rules of Amateur Status

Any person who considers that any action he is proposing to take might endanger his amateur status should submit particulars to the United States Golf Association for consideration.

Definition of an Amateur Golfer

An amateur golfer is one who plays the game as a non-remunerative or non-profit-making sport.

Rule 1 Forfeiture of Amateur Status at Any Age

The following are examples of acts at any age which are contrary to the Definition of an Amateur Golfer and cause forfeiture of amateur status:

1. **Professionalism**

   a. Receiving payment or compensation for serving as a professional golfer or identifying oneself as a professional golfer.

   b. Taking any action for the purpose of becoming a professional golfer.

   Note: Such actions include applying for a professional's position; filing application to a school or competition conducted to qualify persons to play as professionals in tournaments; receiving services from or entering into an agreement, written or oral, with a sponsor or professional agent; agreement to accept payment or compensation for allowing one's name or likeness as a skilled golfer to be used for any commercial purpose; and applying for, holding or retaining membership in any organization of professional golfers.

2. **Playing for Prize Money**

Playing for prize money or its equivalent in a match, tournament or exhibition.

Note: A player may participate in an event in which prize money or its equivalent is offered, provided that prior to participation he irrevocably waives his right to accept prize money in that event. (See USGA Policy on Gambling for definition of prize money.)

3. **Instruction**

Receiving payment or compensation, directly or indirectly, for giving instruction in playing golf, either orally, in writing, by pictures or by other demonstrations, to either individuals or groups.

Exceptions:

1. Golf instruction may be given by an employee of an educational institution or system to students of the institution or system and by camp counselors to those in their charge, provided that the total time devoted to golf instruction during a year comprises less than 50 percent of the time spent during the year in the performance of all duties as such employee or counselor.

2. Payment or compensation may be accepted for instruction in writing, provided one's ability or reputation as a golfer was not a major factor in one's employment or in the commission or sale of one's work.

4. **Prizes, Testimonials and Gifts**

a. Acceptance of a prize or testimonial of the following character (this applies to total prizes

received for any event or series of events in any
one tournament or exhibition, including hole-in-
one or other events in which golf skill is a factor):

  (i) Of retail value exceeding $500; or

  (ii) Of a nature which is the equivalent of
money or makes it readily convertible
into money.

Exceptions:

1. Prizes of only symbolic value (such as metal
trophies).

2. More than one testimonial award may be
accepted from different donors even though
their total retail value exceeds $500, provided
they are not presented so as to evade the $500
value limit for a single award. (Testimonial
awards relate to notable performances or contri-
butions to golf, as distinguished from tournament prizes.)

b. Conversion of a prize into money.

c. Accepting expenses in any amount as a prize.

d. Because of golf skill or golf reputation, accepting
in connection with any golfing event:

  (i) Money, or

  (ii) Anything else, other than merchandise of
nominal value provided to all players.

5. **Lending Name or Likeness**

Because of golf skill or golf reputation, receiving
or contracting to receive payment, compensation
or personal benefit, directly or indirectly, for allowing one's name or likeness as a golfer to be used in

any way for the advertisement or sale of anything, whether or not used in or appertaining to golf, except as a golf author or broadcaster as permitted by Rule 1-7.

6. Personal Appearance

Because of golf skill or golf reputation, receiving payment or compensation, directly or indirectly, for a personal appearance, except that reasonable expenses actually incurred may be received if no golf competition or exhibition is involved.

7. Broadcasting and Writing

Because of golf skill or golf reputation, receiving payment or compensation, directly or indirectly, for broadcasting concerning golf, a golf event or golf events, writing golf articles or books, or allowing one's name to be advertised or published as the author of golf articles or books of which one is not actually the author.

Exceptions:

1. Broadcasting or writing as part of one's primary occupation or career, provided instruction in playing golf is not included except as permitted in Rule 1-3.

2. Part-time broadcasting or writing, provided (a) the player is actually the author of the commentary, articles or books, (b) instruction in playing golf is not included except as permitted in Rule 1-3 and (c) the payment or compensation does not have the purpose or effect, directly or indirectly, of financing participation in a golf competition or golf competitions.

8. **Golf Equipment**

   Because of golf skill or golf reputation, accepting golf balls, clubs, golf merchandise, golf clothing or golf shoes, directly or indirectly, from anyone manufacturing such merchandise without payment of current market price.

9. **Membership and Privileges**

   Because of golf skill or golf reputation, accepting membership or privileges in a club or at a golf course without full payment for the class of membership or privileges involved unless such membership or privileges have been awarded (1) as purely and deservedly honorary, (2) in recognition of an outstanding performance or contribution to golf and (3) without a time limit.

10. **Expenses**

    Accepting expenses, in money or otherwise, from any source other than from a member of the player's family or legal guardian to engage in a golf competition or exhibition, or to improve golf skill.

    Exceptions: A player may receive a reasonable amount of expenses as follows:

    1. AGE RESTRICTIONS

       A player may accept a reasonable amount of expenses to any amateur golf competition or exhibition until (i) the September 1 following graduation from secondary school or (ii) his 19th birthday, whichever shall come first.

    2. TEAM COMPETITIONS

       As a representative of a recognized golf club or

golf association in a team competition between or among golf clubs or golf associations when such expenses are paid by one or more of the golf clubs or golf associations involved or, subject to the approval of the USGA, as a representative in a team competition conducted by some other athletic organization.

3. USGA PUBLIC LINKS CHAMPIONSHIPS

As a qualified contestant in the USGA Amateur Public Links Championships proper, but only within limits fixed by the USGA.

4. SCHOOL, COLLEGE, MILITARY TEAMS

As a representative of a recognized educational institution or of a military service in (1) team events or (2) other events which are limited to representatives of recognized educational institutions or of military services, respectively. In each case, expenses may be accepted from only an educational or military authority.

5. INDUSTRIAL OR BUSINESS TEAMS

As a representative of an industrial or business golf team in industrial or business golf team competitions, respectively, but only within limits fixed by the USGA. (A statement of such limits may be obtained on request from the USGA.)

6. INVITATION UNRELATED TO GOLF SKILL

As a player invited for reasons unrelated to golf skill (e.g., a celebrity, a business associate or customer, a guest in a club-sponsored competition, a winner of a random drawing, etc.) to take part in a golf event or to improve golf skill.

Note 1: Except as otherwise provided in the Exceptions to Rule 1-10, acceptance of expenses from an employer, a partner or other vocational source is not permissible.

Note 2: Business Expenses — It is permissible to play in a golf competition while on a business trip with expenses paid provided that the golf part of the expenses is borne personally and is not charged to business. Further, the business involved must be actual and substantial, and not merely a subterfuge for legitimizing expenses when the primary purpose is golf competition.

Note 3: Private Transport — Acceptance of private transport furnished or arranged for by a tournament sponsor, directly or indirectly, as an inducement for a player to engage in a golf competition or exhibition shall be considered accepting expenses under Rule 1-10.

11. **Scholarships**

Because of golf skill or golf reputation, accepting the benefits of a scholarship or grant-in-aid other than in accord with the regulation of the National Collegiate Athletic Association, the Association of Intercollegiate Athletics for Women, the National Association for Intercollegiate Athletics, or the National Junior College Athletic Association.

12. **Conduct Detrimental to Golf**

Any conduct, including activities in connection with golf gambling, which is considered detrimental to the best interests of the game.

Rule 2 — Advisory Opinions, Enforcement and Reinstatement

1. **Advisory Opinions**

    Any person who considers that any action he is proposing to take might endanger his amateur status may submit particulars to the staff of the United States Golf Association for advice. If dissatisfied with the staff's advice, he may request that the matter be referred to the Amateur Status and Conduct Committee for decision. If dissatisfied with the Amateur Status and Conduct Committee's decision, he may, by written notice to the staff within 30 days after being notified of the decision, appeal to the Executive Committee, in which case he shall be given reasonable notice of the next meeting of the Executive Committee at which the matter may be heard and shall be entitled to present his case in person or in writing. The decision of the Executive Committee shall be final.

2. **Enforcement**

    Whenever information of a possible act contrary to the Definition of an Amateur Golfer by a player claiming to be an amateur shall come to the attention of the United States Golf Association, the staff shall notify the player of the possible act contrary to the Definition of an Amateur Golfer, invite the player to submit such information as the player deems relevant and make such other investigation as seems appropriate under the circumstances. The staff shall submit to the Amateur Status and Conduct Committee all information provided by the player, their findings and their recommendation, and the Amateur Status and Conduct Committee shall decide whether an act contrary to the Definition of an Amateur Golfer has occurred. If dissatisfied with the Amateur Status and Conduct Committee's decision, the player may, by written notice to the staff within 30 days after being notified of the decision, appeal to the Executive Committee, in which case the player shall be given reasonable notice of the next meeting of the Executive Committee at which the matter may be heard and shall be entitled to present his case in person or in writing. The decision of the Executive Committee shall be final.

Upon a final decision of the Amateur Status and Conduct Committee or the Executive Committee that a player has acted contrary to the Definition of an Amateur Golfer, such Committee may require the player to refrain or desist from specified actions as a condition of retaining his amateur status or declare the amateur status of the player forfeited. Such Committee shall notify the player, if possible, and may notify any interested golf association of any action taken under this paragraph.

3. **Reinstatement**

a. AUTHORITY AND PRINCIPLES

Either the Executive Committee or its Amateur Status and Conduct Committee may reinstate a player to amateur status and prescribe the waiting period necessary for reinstatement or deny reinstatement. In addition, the Amateur Status and Conduct Committee may authorize the staff of the USGA to reinstate a player to amateur status and prescribe the waiting period necessary for reinstatement in situations where the acts contrary to the Definition of an Amateur Golfer are covered by ample precedent.

Each application for reinstatement shall be decided on its merits with consideration normally being given to the following principles:

(i) AWAITING REINSTATEMENT

The professional holds an advantage over the amateur by reason of having devoted himself to the game as his profession; other persons acting contrary to the Rules of Amateur Status also obtain advantages not available to the amateur. They do not necessarily lose such advantage merely by deciding to cease acting contrary to the Rules.

Therefore, an applicant for reinstatement to amateur status shall undergo a period awaiting reinstatement as prescribed.

The period awaiting a first reinstatement shall start from the date of the player's last act contrary to the Definition of an Amateur Golfer unless it is decided that it shall start from the date of the player's last known act contrary to the Definition of an Amateur Golfer. The period awaiting a subsequent reinstatement shall start from the date the application arrives at the USGA.

(ii) PERIOD AWAITING REINSTATEMENT

A period awaiting reinstatement of two years normally will be required. However,

that period may *be extended or shortened.*
Longer periods normally will be required
when applicants have played extensively
for prize money, regardless of performance, or have been previously reinstated; shorter periods often will be permitted when applicants have acted
contrary to the Rules for one year or less.
A probationary period of one year normally will be required when an applicant's only act contrary to the Definition
of an Amateur Golfer was to accept a
prize of retail value exceeding $500.

(iii) PLAYERS OF NATIONAL PROMINENCE

Players of national prominence who
have acted contrary to the Definition of
an Amateur Golfer for more than five
years normally will not be eligible for
reinstatement.

(iv) STATUS DURING PERIOD AWAITING
REINSTATEMENT

During the period awaiting reinstatement an applicant for reinstatement shall
conform with the Definition of an Amateur Golfer.

He shall not be eligible to enter competitions limited to amateurs except that
he may enter competitions solely among
members of a club of which he is a member, subject to the approval of the club.
He may also, without prejudicing his
application, enter, as an applicant for
reinstatement, competitions which are

not limited to amateurs but shall not
accept any prize reserved for an amateur.

b. FORM OF APPLICATION

Each application for reinstatement shall be
prepared, in duplicate, on forms provided by the
USGA.

The application must be filed through a recognized amateur golf association in whose district the applicant resides. The association's recommendation, if any, will be considered. If the applicant is unknown to the association, this should be noted and the application forwarded to the USGA, without prejudice.

c. OBJECTION BY APPLICANT

If dissatisfied with the decision with respect to
his application for reinstatement, the applicant
may, by written notice to the staff within 30
days after being notified of the decision, appeal
to the Executive Committee, in which case he
shall be given reasonable notice of the next
meeting of the Executive Committee at which
the matter may be heard and shall be entitled to
present his case in person or in writing. The
decision of the Executive Committee shall be
final.

USGA Policy on Gambling

The Definition of an Amateur Golfer provides that an amateur golfer is one who plays the game as a non-remunerative or non-profit-making sport. When gambling motives are introduced, problems can arise which threaten the integrity of the game.

The USGA does not object to participation in wagering among individual golfers or teams of golfers when participation in the wagering is limited to the players, the players may only wager on themselves or their teams, the sole source of all money won by players is advanced by the players and the primary purpose is the playing of the game for enjoyment.

The distinction between playing for prize money and gambling is essential to the validity of the Rules of Amateur Status. Participation in wagering among individual golfers and participation in wagering among teams constitutes golf wagering and not playing for prize money.

On the other hand, organized amateur events open to the general golfing public and designed and promoted to create cash prizes are not approved by the USGA. Golfers participating in such events without irrevocably waiving their right to cash prizes are deemed by the USGA to be playing for prize money.

The USGA is opposed to and urges its Member Clubs, all golf associations and all other sponsors of golf competitions to prohibit types of gambling such as: (1) Calcuttas, (2) other auction pools, (3) pari-mutuels and (4) any other forms of gambling organized for general participation or permitting participants to bet on someone other than themselves or their teams.

The Association may deny amateur status, entry in

USGA Championships and membership on USGA teams for international competitions to players whose activities in connection with golf gambling, whether organized or individual, are considered by the USGA to be contrary to the best interests of golf.

INDEX
TO THE
RULES OF GOLF

Index to the Rules of Golf

	RULE	PAGE
ABNORMAL GROUND CONDITIONS 25		88
ADDRESSING THE BALL —		
See "BALL, Addressing"		
ADVICE		
Definition. 8		42
Giving or asking for. 8-1		43
ANIMAL, BURROWING, HOLE BY 25		88
Ball moved in search 12-1		51
ARTIFICIAL DEVICES AND		
UNUSUAL EQUIPMENT 14-3		57
ARTIFICIAL OBJECTS 24		84
ASSISTANCE. 14-2		57
BALL		
Addressing:		
Ball moving after address 18-2b		69
Definition 18		67
Assisting play 22		83
Cleaning. 21		82
Damaged, unfit for play 5-3		33
Deflected or stopped. 19		71
Dropped or dropping:		
By whom and how 20-2a		76
Lifting ball wrongly dropped. 20-6		80
Playing dropped ball from wrong place. 20-7		81
Rolling to position where there is		
interference by the condition		
from which relief taken. 20-2c		76
Rolling out of bounds, into a		
hazard, nearer hole, etc. 20-2c		76
Touching player or equipment 20-2a		76
When ball dropped is in play 20-4		80
When to re-drop 20-2c		76
Where to drop 20-2b		76
Embedded. 25-2		93
Local Rule . . . . App. I		119
Exchanging during play of hole. 15-1		60
Exerting influence on 1-2		23
Foreign material applied 5-2		33

	RULE	PAGE

BALL — continued

Holed — definition 16   62

Holing out:

    Ball played from teeing ground. 1-1   23

    Failure, stroke play 3-2   26

Identification:

    Lifting for 12-2   52

    Mark. 6-5   37

    . . . . 12-2, Pre.   52

Influencing position or movement 1-2   23

In motion:

    Deflected or stopped 19   71

    Removing loose impediment

        on line of play 23-1   84

    Removing obstruction

        on line of play 24-1   84

In play — Definition . . . . Defs.   9

Interfering with play. 22   83

Lie:

    Altered 20-3b   78

    Improving. 13-2   54

Lifted or lifting:

    By player without authority. 18-2a   68

    By whom permissible 20-1   75

    Marking position before lifting. 20-1   75

    Putting green 16-1b   63

Lost — See "LOST BALL"

Marking position before lifting 20-1   75

    Local Rule . . . . App. I   119

Moved or moving:

    After address. 18-2b   69

    After loose impediment touched 18-2c   69

    By another ball. 18-5   70

    By fellow-competitor 18-4   70

    By opponent (not in search) 18-3b   70

        Three-ball match 30-2a   103

    By opponent in searching 18-3a   70

    By outside agency. 18-1   68

    By player. 18-2a   68

        Circumstances in which no penalty 18-2a   68

	RULE	PAGE
BALL — continued		
Definition of ball moved 18		67
During swing 14-5		58
In lifting ball under a Rule 20-1		75
In measuring................................ 10-4		48
In removing loose impediment 18-2c		69
In removing movable obstruction 24-1		84
In repairing hole plug or ball mark 16-1c		63
In searching for ball in casual		
water, ground under repair, etc. 12-1		51
In searching for covered ball in hazard 12-1		51
In water in water hazard 14-6		59
Not immediately recoverable .... 18 (Note 1)		67
Playing moving ball 14-5		58
Out of bounds —		
See "OUT OF BOUNDS"		
Overhanging hole 16-2		64
Placed or placing:		
By whom and where 20-3a		78
Fails to come to rest on spot 20-3d		79
Lifting ball wrongly placed 20-6		80
Original lie altered 20-3b		78
Playing placed ball from		
wrong place 20-7		81
Spot not determinable..................... 20-3c		79
When ball placed is in play 20-4		80
Played as it lies 13-1		54
Played from wrong place:		
Match play 20-7a		81
Stroke play 20-7b		81
Playing from where previous stroke played 20-5		80
Provisional ball 27-2		99
Definition 27		98
Resting against flagstick...................... 17-4		66
Searching for............................... 12-1		51
Second ball, stroke play 3-3		26
.... 20-7b		81
Seeing when playing 12-1		51
Specifications:		
Details........................... App. III		155
General 5-1		33

	RULE	PAGE
BALL — continued		
Striking:		
Another ball	19-5	74
Competitor's side	19-2b	73
Fairly	14-1	57
Fellow-competitor's side	19-4	74
Flagstick or attendant	17-3	66
More than once	14-4	58
Opponent's side	19-3	73
Three-ball match	30-2b	103
Outside agency	19-1	72
Player's side	19-2a	73
Substituting another ball during play of hole	15-1	60
Touched:		
By opponent	18-3b	70
By player purposely	18-2a	68
Unfit for play	5-3	33
Unplayable	28	101
Wrong	15	59
Four-ball:		
Match play	30-3d	104
Stroke play	31-6	107
BALL-MARKER		
Moved in process of lifting ball	20-1	75
Moved in process of replacing ball	20-3a	78
Not equipment — See Definition of "Equipment"	Defs.	11
BEST-BALL MATCH	30	103
BOGEY, PAR AND STABLEFORD COMPETITIONS	32	108
BUNKER — See "HAZARD"		
CADDIE		
Breach of Rule by	6-4	36
Definition	Defs.	10
One caddie per player	6-4	36
CART		
Status — See Definition of "Equipment"	Defs.	11
CASUAL WATER	25	88
Ball moved during search	12-1	51

	RULE	PAGE
CLAIMS		
Match play 2-5		25
. . . . 34-1a		115
CLEANING BALL. 21		82
CLUB(S)		
Borrowing or sharing. 4-4b		32
Changing playing characteristics 4-2		31
Damage during play 4-1g		30
Declaring excess club out of play 4-4c		32
Face markings. . . . . App. II		143
Foreign material on face 4-3		31
Form and make 4-1		28
. . . . App. II		143
Grounding:		
In hazard 13-4		55
Lightly 13-2		54
Maximum number allowed 4-4a		31
Placing in hazard. 13-4		55
Replacement during round 4-4a		31
COMMITTEE		
Decision final 34-3		116
Definition . . . . Defs.		10
Duties and powers 33		111
Extending stipulated round to settle tie. 2-3		24
Practice regulations:		
Alteration . . . . 7-1 (Note)		41
	7-2 (Note 2)	42
COMPETITOR		
Definition . . . . Defs.		10
CONCESSION 2-4		24
CONDITIONS		
Committee to lay down. 33-1		111
Matters to include . . . . App. I		119
Draw for match play . . . . App. I		134
Handicap allowances . . . . App. I		135
How to decide ties . . . . App. I		133
Optional conditions . . . . App. I		136
Player responsible for knowing 6-1		35

	RULE	PAGE
COURSE		
Defining bounds and margins 33-2a		111
Definition. . . . . Defs.		11
Unplayable 33-2d		112
DECISIONS		
Committee's powers 34-3		116
Equity 1-4		23
Referee's final 34-2		116
DEFINITIONS . . . . Sec. II		9
DELAY		
Undue 6-7		38
DISCONTINUANCE OF PLAY		
Condition requiring immediate discontinuance . . . . 6-8b(Note)		40
Lifting ball when play discontinued 6-8c		40
Procedure when play suspended by Committee 6-8b		39
When permitted 6-8a		39
DISPUTES 34		115
DISTANCE, GAUGING OR MEASURING 14-3		57
DIVOTS 13-2		54
DORMIE 2-1		24
DOUBT AS TO PROCEDURE, STROKE PLAY 3-3		26
DRAW, GENERAL NUMERICAL . . . . App. I		135
DROPPING BALL —		
See "BALL, Dropped or Dropping"		
EMBEDDED BALL 25-2		93
EQUIPMENT		
Ball at rest moved by. 18		67
Ball in motion deflected or stopped by 19		71
Definition. 18		67
Unusual 14-3		57
EQUITY		
Disputes decided by 1-4		23
ETIQUETTE . . . . Sec. I		3
FELLOW-COMPETITOR		
Definition. . . . . Defs.		11
FLAGSTICK 17		65
Definition. . . . . Defs.		11
Dimensions . . . . App. IV		159
FORECADDIE		
Definition. . . . . Defs.		11

	RULE	PAGE
FOUR-BALL MATCH PLAY 30		103
FOUR-BALL STROKE PLAY 31		106
FOURSOMES 29		102
GAME OF GOLF, Description of. 1-1		23
GENERAL PENALTY		
Match play 2-6		25
Stroke play 3-5		27
GRASS		
Cuttings 25		88
In or bordering bunker, not hazard. 13		53
Touching in finding and identifying ball 12-1		51
Touching with club in hazard 13-4		55
GRIP		
Artificial aid in gripping 14-3		57
Specifications. 4-1c		29
. . . . App. II		148
GROUND UNDER REPAIR. 25-1		89
Ball moved during search 12-1		51
Local Rule — ball drops . . . . App. I		120
GROUPS — See "STROKE PLAY"		
HANDICAP		
Applying, Committee's duty 33-5		113
Duties of player. 6-2		35
Playing off wrong 6-2		35
Knowingly 34-1		115
Stroke table 33-4		113
HAZARD		
Ball lying in or touching 13-4		55
Bunker — definition 13		53
Definition. 13		53
Searching for ball. 12-1		51
Water hazard:		
Ball lying in, relief. 26-1		95
Ball moving in water. 14-6		59
Ball played within:		
Ball comes to rest in hazard. 26-2a		96
Ball lost or unplayable outside		
hazard or out of bounds 26-2b		97
Definitions. 26		94

	RULE	PAGE
HAZARD, continued		
Local Rule:		
Ball drops	App. I	119
Provisional ball	App. I	119
Probing in water during search	12-1	51
HOLE — See also "MATCH PLAY"		
Ball overhanging	16-2	64
Conceding in match play	2-4	24
Damaged	33-2b	111
Definition	Defs.	12
Failure to complete, stroke play	3-2	26
Halved	2-2	24
Made by burrowing animal, etc.	25-1	89
Made by greenkeeper	25	88
New holes for competition	33-2b	111
HONOR	10	46
IDENTIFICATION OF BALL — See "BALL, Identification"		
INFORMATION AS TO STROKES TAKEN	9	44
INTERFERENCE		
By another ball	22	83
Casual water, ground under repair,		
hole made by burrowing animal	25-1a	89
Obstruction	24-2a	85
IRREGULARITIES OF SURFACE	13-2	54
LATERAL WATER HAZARD — See "HAZARD"		
LIE OF BALL — See "BALL, Lie"		
LIFTED OR LIFTING BALL — See "BALL, Lifted or Lifting"		
LIGHTNING	6-8a	39
	App. IV	159
LINE OF PLAY		
Definition	Defs.	13
Improving	13-2	54
Indicating:		
Other than on putting green	8-2a	43
Putting green	8-2b	43
LINE OF PUTT		
Definition	Defs.	13
See "PUTTING GREEN"		
LOCAL RULES		
Committee responsible for	33-8a	114

	RULE	PAGE

LOCAL RULES, continued

Matters to consider .... App. I — 119

Waiving penalty .... 33-8b — 114

LOOSE IMPEDIMENTS

Ball moving after touching.................... 18-2c — 69

Covering ball in hazard .... 12-1 — 51

Definition................................... 23 — 83

Relief .... 23-1 — 84

Removal on line of putt...................... 16-1a — 62

Removal while ball in motion .... 23-1 — 84

LOST BALL

Casual water, ground under repair, etc. .... 25-1c — 91

Definition................................... 27 — 98

Obstruction................................. 24-2c — 87

Procedure .... 27-1 — 99

Water hazard................................ 26-1 — 95

MARKER

Definition................................... Defs. — 14

Recording scores .... 6-6a — 37

  Bogey and par competitions .... 32-1a — 109

  Four-ball stroke play..................... 31-4 — 106

  Stableford competition .... 32-1b — 109

MATCH PLAY

Claims...................................... 2-5 — 25

Combining with stroke play .... 33-1 — 111

Concession of next stroke, hole or match........ 2-4 — 24

Draw .... App. I — 134

Extending stipulated round to settle tie .... 2-3 — 24

General penalty.............................. 2-6 — 25

Discontinuing play by agreement............... 6-8a — 39

Halved hole................................. 2-2 — 24

Handicap .... 6-2a — 35

Matches — See Definition of "Sides and Matches" .... Defs. — 17

Reckoning of holes .... 2-1 — 24

  Winner of:

    Hole....................................... 2-1 — 24

    Match...................................... 2-3 — 24

MATERIAL PILED FOR REMOVAL .... 25 — 88

MEASURING

Artificial device .... 14-3 — 57

Ball moved in .... 10-4 — 48

	RULE	PAGE
OBSERVER		
Definition. . . . . Defs.		15
OBSTRUCTIONS 24		84
Local Rule:		
Ball drops. . . . . App. I		120
Temporary obstructions . . . . App. I		119
ORDER OF PLAY. 10		46
Best-ball and four-ball match play. 30-3c		104
Four-ball stroke play 31-5		106
Threesome or foursome. 29-1		102
OUT OF BOUNDS		
Definition. 27		98
Objects defining are fixed 13-2		54
Are not obstructions 24		84
Procedure 27-1		99
OUTSIDE AGENCY		
Ball at rest moved by 18-1		68
Ball in motion deflected or stopped by 19-1		72
Definition. 19		71
PAR COMPETITIONS. 32		108
PAR COMPUTATION . . . . App. IV		159
PARTNER		
Absence:		
Best-ball and four-ball match play. 30-3a		104
Four-ball stroke play 31-2		106
Definition . . . . Defs.		16
PENALTY		
Agreement to waive 1-3		23
Best-ball and four-ball match play . . . . 30-3e, -3f		105
Cancelled when round cancelled 33-2d		112
Disqualification — waiving,		
modifying or imposing 33-7		114
Four-ball stroke play 31-7,-8		107–108
General:		
Match play 2-6		25
Stroke play 3-5		27
Penalty stroke:		
Definition . . . . Defs.		16
Reporting to opponent or marker 9-2		44
. . . . 9-3		45

	RULE	PAGE
PENALTY, continued		
Time limit on imposition:		
Match play 34-1a		115
Stroke play 34-1b		115
Waiving by Local Rule 33-8b		114
PLACING BALL — See "BALL, Placed or Placing"		
PLAYER, DUTIES OF. 6		35
PLAYING OUT OF TURN 10		46
PRACTICE		
Before or between rounds 7-1		41
During round 7-2		41
Ground 33-2c		112
Swing . . . . 7-2 (Note 1)		42
"PREFERRED LIES" AND "WINTER RULES" . . . . . App. I		130
PROTECTION FROM ELEMENTS 14-2		57
PROVISIONAL BALL 27-2		99
Definition. 27		98
Local Rule for water hazard. App. I		120
Teeing ground. 10-3		48
PUTTING GREEN		
Ball:		
Cleaning. 16-1b		63
Lifting. 16-1b		63
Overhanging hole 16-2		64
Conceding opponent's next stroke. 2-4		24
Definition. 16		62
Line of putt:		
Pointing out 8-2b		43
Position of caddie or partner 16-1f		64
Standing astride or on 16-1e		63
Touching 16-1a		62
Playing stroke while another ball in motion. 16-1g		64
Repair of hole plugs, ball marks and other damage. . . . 16-1c		63
Testing surface 16-1d		63
Wrong putting green. 25-3		93
REFEREE		
Decision final 34-2		116
Definition. . . . . Defs.		16
Limiting duties 33-1		111

	RULE	PAGE
ROADS AND PATHS		
When obstruction —		
See Definition of "Obstruction"	Defs.	15
RUB OF THE GREEN		
Definition	Defs.	17
RULE(S)		
Agreement to waive	1-3	23
Definition.	Defs.	17
Information on not advice	8	42
Points not covered.	1-4	23
Rectification of serious breach, stroke play.	20-7b	81
Refusal to comply, stroke play.	3-4	27
Waiving.	33-1	111
SCORER — See "MARKER"		
SCORES AND SCORE CARDS		
Committee's responsibility	33-5	113
Competitor's responsibility	6-6b	37
. . . .	6-6d	37
Four-ball stroke play	31-4	106
Marker's responsibility.	6-6a	37
Four-ball stroke play	31-4	106
No alteration after return.	6-6c	37
Wrong score	6-6d	37
SECOND BALL		
Order of play on teeing ground	10-3	48
Played when in doubt as to procedure	3-3	26
Played when serious breach may be involved	20-7b	81
SIDES AND MATCHES		
Definitions	Defs.	17
SLOW PLAY.	6-7	38
Condition modifying penalty in stroke play	6-7(Note)	38
STABLEFORD COMPETITIONS	32	108
STANCE		
Astride or touching line of putt	16-1e	63
Building	13-3	55
Definition.	18	67
Fairly taking	13-2	54
Interference with by:		
Casual water, ground under repair, etc.	25-1a	89
Immovable obstruction	24-2a	85

	RULE	PAGE
STANCE, continued		
Out of bounds	27	98
Outside teeing ground	11-1	49
STIPULATED ROUND		
Definition	Defs.	18
STROKE		
Assistance:		
Artificial devices	14-3	57
Physical assistance	14-2	57
Protection from elements	14-2	57
Conceding	2-4	24
Definition	14	57
Playing from where previous stroke played	20-5	80
Striking ball more than once	14-4	58
STROKE PLAY		
Combining with match play	33-1	111
Doubt as to procedure	3-3	26
Failure to hole out	3-2	26
General penalty	3-5	27
Groups:		
Changing	6-3b	36
Committee to arrange	33-3	113
New holes	33-2b	111
Refusal to comply with Rule	3-4	27
Scores — See "SCORES AND SCORE CARDS"		
Winner	3-1	26
SUSPENSION OF PLAY	33-2d	112
Procedure for players	6-8b	39
TEEING GROUND		
Ball falling off tee	11-3	49
Creating or eliminating irregularities	13-2	54
Definition	11	49
Order of play:		
Match play	10-1a	46
Stroke play	10-2a	47
Threesome or foursome	29-1	102
Playing outside	11-4	50
Provisional or second ball from	10-3	48
Standing outside to play ball within	11-1	49
Teeing ball	11-1	49
Tee-markers — status	11-2	49
Wrong teeing ground	11-5	50

	RULE	PAGE
THREE-BALL MATCHES 30		103
THREESOME. 29		102
THROUGH THE GREEN		
Definition. . . . . Defs.		18
TIES		
Extending stipulated round to settle, match play 2-3		24
How and when decided. 33-6		114
Recommendation. . . . . App. I		133
TIME OF STARTING		
Committee's responsibility 33-3		113
Condition modifying penalty. . . . . 6-3 (Note)		36
Player's responsibility. 6-3a		36
TOUCHING BALL —		
See "BALL, Touched"		
TURF, CUT, PLACED IN POSITION. 13-2		54
UNDUE DELAY 6-7		38
UNPLAYABLE BALL 28		101
WATER HAZARD — See "HAZARD"		
"WINTER RULES" . . . . App. I		130
WRONG BALL. 15		59
Four-ball match play 30-3d		104
Four-ball stroke play 31-6		107
Time spent in playing — See Definition		
of "Lost Ball" . . . . Defs.		14
WRONG INFORMATION		
As to strokes taken in match play. 9-2		44
Voids time limit for claim 2-5		25
. . . . 34-1		115
WRONG PLACE		
Ball played from 20-7		81
Lifting ball dropped or placed at 20-6		80
WRONG SCORE. 6-6d		37